THIS IS YOUR CAPTAIN SPEAKING!

by Walt and Ann Bohrer

Cover Art and Cartoons
by
Bob Stevens

AERO PUBLISHERS, INC.

329 Aviation Road Fallbrook, Cal. 92028

Library of Congress Cataloging in Publication Data

Bohrer, Walt.
   This is your captain speaking!

   1. Aeronautics--Anecdotes, facetiae, satire, etc.
2. Air travel--Anecdotes, facetiae, satire, etc.
I. Bohrer, Ann, joint author. II. Title.
HE9777.B6   387.7'02'07   74-31054
ISBN 0-8168-9000-5

Printed and Published in the United States by Aero Publishers, Inc.

FOREWORD

I have personally known the brother-sister flying-writing team of Walt and Ann Bohrer since 1926, and over this seemingly interminable span of forty years-plus I have noted it was always they who were ferreting out aviation's zany happenings rather than its more serious events. In fact, I had always thought that some day in the future, if enough of these humorous happenings could be put together, the result would be a humorous book. I am happy to say this has come to pass, not only in this book slanted to airline happenings, but in previous books involving aviation generally.

To make my point, Ann and Walt were on hand at the opening of the Pacific Coast airmail service by Vern Gorst and his Pacific Air Transport (PAT), a predecessor of United Air Lines, at Vancouver, Washington, in 1926, and while the run-of-the-mill aviation scribes of the day were noting the time made by the intrepid airmail pilots arriving from the north and the south in their little Ryan M-1 monoplanes, it was only they who noted that pilot Heber Miller had split the seat of his flying suit wide open at the seam while attempting to disengage his elongated carcass from the cramped M-1 cockpit. They also noted that more powerful engines than the 200-horsepower Wright J4 were needed for airmail planes, not because of the mail loads, but because of the weight of such pilots as Vern Bookwalter who was affectionately known as "Anti-lift"!

This sense—or nonsense—of humor soon got the Bohrers the job of writing aviation news and features for Western Flying magazine, a major aviation publication of the period, a stint they stuck with for a score of years, forever sprinkling their items and features with an abundance of sparkling humor to the great delight of Western Flying's readers, such as the following item clipped from an early issue of that magazine:

> Ever since **Joe Harrell**, pilot of a Travelrock at the Eugene Airport, snapped off a fence post at the south end of the field in a most astounding fashion, he has been the champeen aerial fence post snapper of the county, all of which made **Clarence Saville**, a pilot over in the rival city of Springfield, across the tracks, very unhappy. So, in order to show up that "blinkin' smart-aleck, Harrell," Saville piles into his ship and scours the countryside for a nize fence to try out on. Finally finding one, he landed and looked the posts over to see if they were worth busting. Satisfied they were better posts than Joe's, he climbed back into his ship and opened her up. At exactly three feet elevation he got one post very neatly, right on the button, but a sudden sinking sensation (probably a settle-draft) caused him to suddenly lose altitude when lo and behold! four more posts appeared right in front of his lower wing! Saville is not only the new champeen fence post snapper of the county, but is also the champeen piece picker-upper of 18 townships, having spent the

next two days picking up his ship and putting it into little sacks. And as for Harrell, he's out looking over a row of telegraph poles!

Also in 1926, Walt, together with Tex Rankin, the late famed acrobatic champion from whom Walt was taking flying lessons in a Curtiss Jenny and with whom he was to be closely associated for the next 22 years, started a unique hand-lettered, mimeographed aviation gossip sheet entitled "Tale Spins", featuring the slogan, "The Monkey Glands of Aviation", which indeed it turned out to be! In "Tale Spins" they good-naturedly lambasted Rankin employees and other local flying gentry for fare-thee-well, each item profusely illustrated with Walt's cartoons. I, myself, came in for a bit of drubbing in one issue beneath the heading: "Elrey Jeppesen—Who, When, Where, Why and How!", all of which was seemingly satisfactorily answered except the "Why", for which, apparently, no answer could be found.

Typical of the "Tale Spins" features was a well-illustrated story describing in fierce detail a "new and powerful" aircraft engine supposedly invented by Danny Grecco, well known pilot-mechanic, and former aerial daredevil of the Portland, Oregon, area. Dubbed the "Odor Motor", this amazing engine derived its awesome and overwhelming power from the locked-in, non-escapable odor of limburger cheese—without a doubt the very first scent of the coming jet age. Another story told "How Aeroncas Were Born", indicating in vivid detail that they had come from the infinite depths of outer space not unlike a plague of locusts!

Later, with sister, Ann, as "co-pilot", Tale Spins was carried on as a monthly magazine for better than ten years boasting among its paid subscribers such aviation personalities as Admiral Byrd; Frank Hawks; Eddie Rickenbacker; Amelia Earhart; Will Rogers and many others.

Ann, who had taken her first flight with Vance Breese in 1923, continued her flying lessons while working for and barnstorming with Tex Rankin and his crew of instructor-pilots (of which I was one for a time). She soloed in 1928 and continued her flying by working for Hans Mirow, a Portland flying school operator who later became a well-known Alaskan bush pilot, and with a long office stint with the Eyerly Aircraft Company of Salem, Oregon. During this period, Ann was named official airport hostess and greeter for the city of Salem, Oregon's state capital. Walt remained with Rankin through World War II at his Air Force contract primary training facility at Tulare, California, and until Tex's untimely death in 1947. Both have been writing aviation stories ever since.

Thus, with all of this experience in flying, writing and meeting the cream of the flying crop under their belts, what could be more natural for the Bohrers than to turn out such books as this?

I, therefore, am elated to have been chosen to write this Foreword, not only because of my personal love of flying and aviation humor, but because the book features airline captains, the very people it has been my great pleasure to serve with Jeppesen flight aids for lo, these many years! And, as you peruse the ensuing pages of THIS IS YOUR CAPTAIN SPEAKING, two things may occur to you: (1) that I was justified in extolling the Bohrer's sense of humor, and (2) perhaps one or two other flight aids should have been developed by the Jeppesen company to pre-warn captains or flight crew members of approaching embarrassing situations, practical jokes, or other forms of miserable mayhem!

E. B. "Jepp" Jeppesen

PREFACE

When the idea of this book first bubbled up in our collective minds, we decided the logical first step would be to tackle one or two unsuspecting airline captains and ask them:

"Have you ever had any funny experiences while flying?"

For some unfathomable reason we pounced first on United Air Lines Captain Frank L. Swaim, probably because he was unfortunate enough to be the first to walk into our clutches.

He unhesitatingly came up with a few experiences he thought were funny, and which we thought were funny, and which we trust you'll think are funny. And with that in mind for starters, we pass a couple on to you:

Captain Swaim, deadheading (flying gratis as a passenger from one company station to another) between Denver and Chicago, happened to be seated directly across from an extremely nervous dowager-type woman who quite obviously had fortified herself with an over-consumption of "Old Panther". During the cruise portion of the flight, one of the engines backfired a time or two when a gas tank had run dry and a slight delay occurred in switching to a full tank. The jittery gal stared goggle-eyed at the backfiring and bucking engine for a second or two, then in a voice clearly audible to all passengers, deaf ones included, she exploded:

"RUN, YOU SON OF A BITCH! KEEP ON RUNNING!"

On yet another occasion Captain Swaim, again deadheading, happened to be sitting in the lounge of a DC-6B, an eight-passenger compartment. The other occupants were a middle-aged couple with a child, obviously born late in life and more than a little spoiled. The embryo juvenile delinquent was constantly interfering with the stewardess performing her duties with no hint of a reprimand from either doting parent. Finally, in sheer desperation and well within earshot of the parents, the stewardess turned on the little monster and said:

"Why don't you go *outside* and play!"

Here were two spontaneous and humorous happenings involving the same captain and the same airline. By this criterion, we thought, what sort of a conglomerate of stories could we get from a *lot* of captains on a *lot* of airlines? So we started delving further into the project and the more we delved the zanier some of the stories got until we came to two conclusions: (1) some airline captains are crazier than people, and (2) if their stories were strung together in some semblance of disorder, they would make one HIGH-larious book—this one!

Now all humorous or oddball incidents don't necessarily take place *on* airliners. Many kooky things develop otherwise, such as between airline crews and control tower people. This one happened at Chicago:

A control tower operator at O'Hare Airport was startled out of ten years' growth one evening when this urgent request burst from the speaker:

"This is Midwest Flight 203. I have only three gallons of fuel left. Request instructions. Over!"

The control tower man leaped out of his seat and grabbed the microphone. "Tower to Midwest Flight 203", he shouted. "Now listen! Stay calm, don't get excited, and, above all, don't panic! Now carefully tell me: what is your exact location? Over."

After a pause that seemed like a century, the voice of the Midwest captain came over the speaker:

"Ah, I'm parked on the runway. I was wondering where the fuel truck was."

Another sparkling bit of conversation between captain and control tower was prompted by the fact that a number of careless pilots have had to pay out of their own pockets for airport boundary lights they had run into and broken while taxiing their airliners from the runways to the terminal building.

On this occasion a United Air Lines pilot, taxiing between a row of boundary lights, called the tower:

"Flight 454 to tower. How high are these boundary lights?"

"About $84.00 apiece!" came the impacting answer from the tower.

Needless to say, no lights were broken and pilots became a bit more wary in taxiing their ships thereafter.

Crazy things often take place in the terminal building even before an airliner or an airline crew is involved. Problems evolve at times even from the most insignificant things. Who, for instance, would believe that the three-lettered code used on airline baggage tags and officially dubbed "designators" (such as LAX for Los Angeles or PDX for Portland) would ever cause any trouble? It did! A rather obese woman boarding a plane at SFO (San Francisco) for Fresno literally "blew her stack" when the agent stamped her tag: FAT, which naturally meant Fresno Air Terminal.

We don't have to point out that the Fresno designator was shortly thereafter changed from FAT to FNO!

In perusing these chapters you will find that the episodes include the entire gamut of airliners from the Fokkers and Ford tri-motors of the '20's and '30's to the modern jets of today, and we want to thank the various personnel of those lines, active or retired, for helping to supply the ridiculous happenstances in the ensuing pages.

With this, we wish you happy reading!

Walt and Ann Bohrer

*   *   *   *   *   *   *   *   *   *   *   *   *   *   *   *   *   *   *

DEDICATION

To our late dear friend, Captain Richard P. (Dick) Craine, and to the host of other airline and airmail pilots it has been our privilege and pleasure to know, we proudly dedicate this book.

ACKNOWLEDGMENTS

Grateful acknowledgement is given to: AIR-ALPES, Michel Ziegler; AIR BAHAMA, Everett W. Terry, Chief Pilot & Assistant Director of Operations; AIR MAIL PIONEERS NEWS; AIR NEW ZEALAND, Captain Geoffrey M. White; AMERICAN AIRLINES, Captain Forest M. Johnston; ANSETT AIRLINES OF PAPUA NEW GUINEA, Captain John W. Kessey; BRANIFF INTERNATIONAL, Mrs. Pat Zahrt, Director of Publications; BRITISH OVERSEAS AIRWAYS CORPORATION, Brian Twomey, Press Officer; BOAC News; CANADIAN PACIFIC AIR, R. A. Keith, Director of Public Relations (1971), Pilot C. E. Ambrose, J. R. Moir, Public Relations Manager (1973); CATHAY PACIFIC AIRWAYS, Peter Waitt, Public Relations; DELTA AIR LINES, F. J. Schwaemmle, Miss Harriette Speer, Public Relations Department; EAST AFRICAN INTERNATIONAL AIRLINE OF AFRICA, J. K. Mwai, Public Relations Manager; EASTERN AIR LINES, Captain Thomas E. Zinn, James R. Ashlock, Director—Field Public Relations; EL AL ISRAEL AIRLINES, Michael Porter, Editor, Public Relations Magazines; FINNAIR, Carl J. Nyberg, General Manager/North America; Veli Virkkunen, Chief Public Relations, Helsinki; HUGHES AIRWEST, Captain Patrick E. O'Grady, Don Gooding, Lee Pitt, Director of Public Relations, Larry Litchfield, Public Relations;

IBERIA AIR LINES OF SPAIN, Anatole Yudin, Manager Customer Relations; I. Sidoli, Public Relations; KLM ROYAL DUTCH AIRLINES, Richard G. Pratt, Public Relations Representative, USA, F. Zandvliet, Head Air Education (Netherlands); LOGANAIR, Captain A. D. Alsop; LUFTHANSA, Neville Kitto, Public Relations Director; NEW ZEALAND NATIONAL AIRWAYS CORPORATION (NAC), Arthur Feslier, Public Relations Manager; NORTHWEST AIRLINES, Captain Mal B. Freeburg, Captain Joe E. Kimm, William L. Pollock, Public Relations; PAN AMERICAN WORLD AIRWAYS, Willard March, Public Relations, Captain Basil Lee Rowe, Captain Richard N.Ogg;

REEVE ALEUTIAN AIRWAYS, Janice Reeve Ogle, Chief Stewardess, "The Williwaw", Reeve News Bulletin; SABENA BELGIAN WORLD AIRLINES, F. Van den Broecke, A.B.P.N.L. President, Herman Michielse, Public Relations Manager; TRANS-CANADA AIR LINES, Fred Fraser, Supervisor, Press Services (1963), Captain G. Lothian; TRANS WORLD AIRLINES, R. H. Helmer, Assistant to Vice President, Public Relations, Captain John A. Guglielmetti; UNITED AIR LINES, Captain G. C. Kehmeier, Captain H. A. Gurney, Captain Frank L. Swaim, Captain Richard P. Craine, Captain Walter "Doc" Eefsen, Zay Smith, Captain E. Hamilton Lee, Captain R. John Wisda, Marvin R. Thompson, Manager of Advertising Services, Captain Harold W. Burlingame, E. "Brownie" Gray, via RUPA Newsletter, Captain George Howson, Retired Secretary of UAL Retired United Pilots Ass'n., Wallace H. Leland, United Newsletter: RUPA (Retired United Pilots Association), J. A. Kennedy, Richard C. Fernald; WESTERN AIRLINES, Captain T. G. "Jerry" Keeley, Sydney J. Albright, Public Relations Manager, Forrest R. Mulvane, WAL News Bureau, "Flight Time" bulletin;

TABLE OF CONTENTS

Pan-Am Boeing Stratocruiser.

Problem Passengers

Airline problem passengers are precisely as they are categorized—problem passengers. Some are merely the icky-picky variety while others are those who discover a mole hill upon boarding and somehow manage to make a mountain of it before deplaning. Not all problem passengers are human, however, for as you shall see, our animal friends, too, manage to kick up a few airwaves of their own. Fortunately most of these problems, human or animal, are minor and wind up as good belly laughs for passengers and/or crew rather than anything serious. Most of the following fall into this category.

An excellent example of "whereof we speak" was the day several years back when Captain Richard N. Ogg of Pan American World Airways was cruising along over the South Pacific in a Boeing Stratocruiser with a twin-deck-load of passengers. Since the bulky Stratocruiser's cabins were

11

Pan-Am Captain Richard N. (Dick) Ogg
believes some passengers would even stoop to
taking their own sonar on a submarine.
(Pan-Am Photo)

somewhat difficult to pressurize in warm climates without
becoming too warm for passenger comfort, some of the Pan-
Am pilots would announce over the plane's intercom system
that the cabin pressure was equivalent to an altitude of 3,000
feet when, actually, it was more like 7,000 or 8,000.

On this particular occasion, Captain Ogg had just completed announcing that although they were flying 14,000 feet
over the Pacific, the air pressure within the cabin was
equivalent to a comfortable 3,000 feet. He had barely hung up
his microphone when a stewardess burst into the pilots' compartment exclaiming, "I've got a passenger back there who
says the pressure isn't *either* 3,000 feet—it's 7,000!"

Somewhat taken aback, Ogg inquired, "How come *he*
knows so all-fired much?"

"Well," was her startling reply, "he has *his own* altimeter
with him, that's why!"

Delta Air Lines Convair "400".

Sure enough, this overly-suspicious passenger had brought along his personal altimeter! Which only goes to show, declares Ogg, that Lincoln was right—you can't fool all of the people all of the time. Or even some of the time!

* * *

Airlines had better check their captains and first officers because some of them *could* be Russian spies!

This bit of "intelligence," or lack of it, was brought to the attention of Delta Air Lines Captain Dave Thayer while on a northbound Convair 440 flight to Chicago.

He had made his regular Little Rock stop and was visiting the Little Rock terminal's men's room. One of his passengers, a portly fiftyish gent, rather excitedly told him he had just offered another passenger—a sailor— a drink from his bottle, and the sailor had, of all things, declined this proffered bit of libation. The portly gent further explained he had then asked the sailor if he was going to Great Lakes and the reply was, "No, I'm going to Chicago." The passenger then explained to

Delta Air Lines Captain Dave Thayer. A Russian spy aboard? Never!(Delta Air Lines Photo)

Thayer that he had FBI connections and was in a position to know that Russia was supplying agents with U.S. Navy uniforms. He was of the determined opinion that *no* U.S. sailor would refuse a drink and that *any* sailor would know that Great Lakes Naval Base was in Chicago. He therefore strongly suggested that Captain Thayer have the culprit promptly removed from the flight and have him investigated.

Upon reboarding the ship a short time later, Captain Thayer's co-pilot, Al Durham, sat down and said, "Guess what? I was just in the men's room and some fat guy offered me a drink and asked if I was going to Great Lakes. I said, 'No, to Chicago'."

Thayer almost fell out of his seat when he realized that, because of Delta's Navy-type uniforms, his co-pilot had been suspected of being a Russian spy!

Airline captains are usually the epitomy of patience but there are times when such effort pushes them to the breaking point. United Air Lines Captain Richard P. (Dick) Craine was one who learned the meaning of the word— a rough 30 minutes in which he didn't only get to the breaking point but to the snapping point, as well.

The incident occurred as members of a large lei-bedecked tour group, still bubbling with excitement over their gala stay in the land of the hula, boarded a United Air Lines DC-8, captained by UAL's senior pilot Craine, for the mainland. In the excitement of final gabfests, everyone became so mixed up in the crowd that husbands, wives and traveling companions became completely separated from each other. This created a real problem since all desired to sit beside their mates or close friends to reminisce on the events of their trip. To make matters worse, DC-8 coach seating arrangements being three seats per side, by the time a passenger had located two seats together, he or she couldn't find his or her partner; usually one was in the fore part of the ship while the other was at the extreme tail end. This called for some quick leg work through the DC-8's cabin to locate the missing one before the seats were gone but invariably the foot race ended in a milling traffic jam in the aisles that would have easily defied the agility of the most streamlined rodent. In the ensuing melee few managed to get seated, despite the efforts of the stewardesses, as by the time the passengers had found their partners, either one or both of the seats previously available had been taken. Then the search for two seats together began all over again, sometimes resulting in the couples again being split up.

The stewardesses, magnificently cloaking their vexation, requested everyone to stay put until seats were located for them but in spite of their pleas the passengers insisted upon turning it into a do-it-yourself project. Noting it was now past take-off time, the stewardesses realized they simply had to get them seated, together or otherwise, but most remained adamant about sitting anywhere but with a certain person—cer-

The late United Air Lines Captain Richard P. (Dick) Craine, to whom, with anonymous others, this book is dedicated. As you will see, Captain Craine, too, had his "go around" with problem passengers.
(United Air Lines Photo)

tainly not in one of the single seats "left over." Eventually, in desperation, one of the harassed stewardesses went forward to the pilots' quarters.

"Will you please come out and help me, Captain Craine?" she asked. "We simply can't get them to sit down— the seats don't come out even to suit them!"

By now the pilots, too, were exasperated at the too-long delay in take-off but they could not while their charges were running helter-skelter like a swarm of ants.

In the hopes of expediting matters, Captain Craine suggested the stewardess call the passenger agent who was an expert in these matters. Craine was certain this would bring about their immediate salvation.

Hastening off, the stewardess secured the agent; however he was no more successful than she in pacifying the passengers. Ordinarily, travelers would accept the inevitable in such situations in good grace but this was not an ordinary group of tourists. These beflowered passengers were still bathed in excitement and could hardly contain themselves until they could blow off steam in a talking binge with their mates or pals. Having to be separated by the tri-seated arrangement in the plane therefore was wholly "for the birds." Consequently the agent's efforts insured nothing but added pandemonium!

When after several more minutes, the pilots still had not received clearance for take-off, Captain Craine looked into the cabin. He had hoped that between the stewardesses and the passenger agent, the difficulties had been straightened out but to his amazement, he found everything was still in the bedlam stage. He could see them checking seats and figured that surely they soon would be successful in juggling a few passengers to everyone's satisfaction. Deciding to stretch his patience a bit further, Craine shut the control room door.

After a few minutes, he took another look to check what progress had been made but found little or no improvement in the situation. His usual serenity was fast ebbing. He thought if he stepped out into the cabin and gave some of the passengers a hard look, perhaps they would take the hint and get themselves seated; however those few who did see him, merely glared back hostilely. Disgustedly Craine re-entered the control room and hoped for the best which had better be quick. He'd about had it.

After an additional 10-minute delay, Craine cast another glance into the cabin and noted the milling around had not subsided one whit. In fact, it appeared arguments were now in progress as well, with the stewardesses and passenger agent acting as referees.

Craine looked at his watch and noted it was now 40 minutes past take-off time. He had experienced delays before but never such a lengthy one and never for such a stupid reason. This was just about the limit—also of his endurance.

Jumping to his feet, Craine aimed for the tourists' section. There was menace in each stride and wrath mirrored in his

United Airlines DC-8-61 flying past Waikiki.

eyes. As he reached the passengers, he found one of the outstanding "performers" of the group was a lei-bedecked
planter-punched man who stood poutingly but firmly in the aisle and avowed he would not go if he could not sit with his
wife. Craine, who was born a kind and gentle soul was no
longer recognizable as such. Planting himself squarely in front
of the spouting human Vesuvius, he addressed everyone as
calmly as he could with these carefully measured words:
"Can't we *possibly* resolve this thing or shall we cancel this
flight?" Craine then turned on his heel, slammed shut the control room door, folded his arms and stared wrathfully at the
instrument board. The first officer asked what luck he'd had
but Craine had come to the point of no-answer. He was battling an immense urge to slam open the control room door and
shout, *"Get to hell in your seats, dammit!"* at the top of his
voice. Only the fact that he was not the type to use profane
language saved the unrully passengers from getting that un-
cheerful earful!

To this day the stewardesses and passenger agent have not been able to determine if it was Craine's anger-rapt countenance, his vibrant personality which defied any opposition, or just his sudden and unexpected approach, but the passengers somehow got themselves seated in a hurry—and, believe us, not necessarily together!

* * *

There are times when just one passenger can do an equally devastating amount of damage to a pilot's otherwise pleasant disposition, and once again United Air Lines Captain Dick Craine was the star of a pre-take-off drama.

The setting was one of which he dubbed his Hawaiian "milk run," and, as usual, Captain Craine was in a happy frame of mind as he proceeded from cabin to flight deck. He had progressed but a few steps when he was stopped short by an attractive, well-dressed young woman who commenced triggering several rapid-fire questions to engage him in conversation. After a minute it was obvious she wasn't particularly interested in the answers. Further, it also was apparent from her speech that she had been enjoying an over-abundance of liquid refreshments. Since he could not prolong the conversation, he smilingly excused himself and turned toward his "office" but the young woman, bubbling with spirits, was not the type to readily terminate the tete-a-tete. She now announced publicly that she was ready to visit the cockpit.

Craine blinked. His ensuing eyebrow-raised "I beg your pardon?" was not a query, as he had understood her perfectly. It was a spontaneous utterance evoked by her startling statement.

The woman rose from her seat and repeated her statement that she would now visit the cockpit.

"Oh, I'm sorry," began Craine, "but you can't do that! It's against company rules."

The woman, however, was playing it deaf. Reaching for the captain's arm, she attempted to determinedly shove him toward the control room.

Craine braced himself. "As I said," he began, "I just *can't* let you do that! It's against the rules!"

"But just for this once, can't you forget the rules?" she cajoled. The hand on his arm continued to pressure him toward the flight deck.

Craine's usually polite smile became strained. He was beginning to feel a little hot around the region of his ears, especially since he noted other passengers nearby were fascinated with the conversation and no doubt more than a little interested in the outcome of this little drama of passenger versus pilot. Craine realized, too, that in this woman's inebriated condition, it would be necessary to exercise considerable firmness. He therefore carefully explained the federal and company regulations prohibiting passengers from entering the flight deck, but he might just as well have talked to the walls because all the while the woman kept insisting and shoving.

Craine, a tall man, was not easily shoved, especially when his feet refused to budge one inch. Patiently he reiterated for what he hoped would be the last time, as he began to feel like a parrot, the reasons why she could *not* visit the pilots' quarters but the results were the same. The hand on his arm continued its attempt to push him in the direction of the control room, indicating that although she had lost some of her senses, one was not her sense of direction.

The captain's smile had by now gone with the wind and his watch told him time was doing likewise. He could not afford to waste any further time; besides the other passengers were now openly staring. Looking sternly at this stubborn passenger, he said, "Look, I could lose my license if I allowed you on the flight deck and I am sure you wouldn't want that to happen to me!"

The exasperating female tossed her head. "I don't *care* about your old license," she spat. "All I want to do is *visit the cockpit!*"

20

"That, madam, is against the rules," finalized Craine, and with an "I'm very sorry" and a polite adios touch of his cap, swung on his heels and strode hastily toward the flight deck, all the while wondering if he were being followed. He wasn't and the ordeal was ended.

With a relieved "*Whew!*," he took his seat beside the first officer. He had, fortunately, finally "gotten through" to her!

* * *

Eastern Air Lines Flight 60 was 30 minutes out of New Orleans en route to New York City, cruising at 33,000 feet, indicating .82 mach. The early morning skies were clear and smooth. Captain Herbert (Smokey) Stover was in command, assisted by Flight Engineer Mike Guerin and First Officer Tom Zinn.

"The routine of the cockpit was suddenly broken by a quiet thumping sound which grew in intensity until it could be felt through the soles of our feet," stated Zinn.

"Smokey and I looked at each other and spoke almost simultaneously: 'Do you hear and feel that thumping?'

"A quick check of all instruments showed everything normal. Smokey grabbed the throttles and gently pulled them back. The aircraft slowed to 280 knots. The mysterious thumping continued.

"Perhaps the landing gear doors were drooping into the slipstream. The remedy didn't help. The throttles were advanced and the large fans in the front of each engine were carefully synchronized. No luck. We decided it must be an access door sprung loose or a fluttering control panel on the wings or tail.

"The thumping continued at a constant 140 beats per minute for about 20 minutes. Then as quickly as the noise started, it stopped.

"We called ahead to our maintenance personnel in New York to have them standing by to check all control surfaces and access doors. An uneventful approach and landing were

One instance when "thumping must have gone wrong" can be attested to by Eastern Air Lines Captains Herbert F. (Smokey) Stover, Jr., above, and Thomas E. Zinn, below. (Eastern Air Lines Photo)

made at Kennedy airport with the questions still in our minds. What was the cause of the noise? Had we done everything we could to solve the mystery? Why had the noise stopped?

"As we pondered these questions the senior stewardess came into the cockpit. 'Boy, do we have a weird passenger on this flight!'

" 'What happened, honey?'

" 'Well, this guy locked himself in the forward lavatory, stripped down, and jogged for 20 minutes in there!' "

The stewardess could never quite figure out why both captain and first officer wanted to kiss her after that bit of kooky information.

* * *

During the dawn of scheduled airline service, in the mid-1920s, the activities of some flying crews were almost legendary; perhaps because they felt it was expected of them. Two such characters who often flew as a team with Imperial Airways, which became BOAC during World War II, were Captain Robert MacIntosh and Flight Mechanic Charles Pearson.

Captain MacIntosh became known as "All Weather Mac" because of his exploits, which included being the first to ever make a commercial landing in fog at Croydon Aerodrome,

Line-up of Imperial Airways Airliners at Croydon Aerodrome, London, 1928.

south of London, in the early twenties. Pearson earned the nickname of "Charlie 'I'll get you home' Pearson" because of a similar contempt for the elements.

One murky evening in April 1925, when even the birds were walking, a man in full evening dress arrived at Croydon insisting on getting to Paris in a hurry. The last flight of the day had gone and he was prepared to pay £50 to any pilot willing to fly to Paris.

The weather was worsening by the minute and no pilot would accept the offer—that is, not until "All Weather Mac" arrived out of the low rain clouds with the 4:00 p.m. flight from Paris.

Handley-Page Airliner of Imperial Airways, 1928, now British Airways.

The duty officer of Imperial Airways asked Mac if he would take the man on a charter flight to Paris; at least to the French coast if weather did not permit getting all the way to Paris. Mac, with his usual disregard for atmospheric conditions, was perfectly willing to return to "Gay Paree" if someone else who enjoyed the (quote) beauties (unquote) of this night's weather would accompany him. Naturally the someone else Mac was referring to was his old pal, Charlie, to whom he offered to share the £50 if Pearson would agree to fly with him. Seeing no plausible reason for not accompanying Mac, Pearson readily, even happily, agreed to go.

A short time later they were battling their way to France without a break in the pea-soup fog. The weather by now had really become a formidable adversary and, as they hugged the waves of the English Channel, this £50 Paris idea was not nearly as appealing as it had been.

As night arrived before Paris, they were forced to land at Le Touquet a short distance from the big city. The two weary crew lads lost no time checking into a hotel for some much-needed shut-eye while their rearin'-to-go passenger went off to gamble at the famous Paris Plage Casino.

At daybreak the next morning, Mac and Pearson found their passenger sleeping, still in his evening dress, under the wing of the DH50 aircraft—a bottle of champagne in each overcoat pocket and two more in his top hat.

Imperial Airways De Havilland 50 aircraft.

Finally, at Paris, Mac escorted their dashingly attired passenger through customs to collect the £50. At that moment two men came forward and slapped handcuffs on the passenger. They were Scotland Yard detectives who divulged the disquieting news that in a few hours they would be taking their captive back to London on the Imperial Airways flight.

Mac and Charlie subsequently learned their passenger had posed as a Polish Count and persuaded a well-known London jeweler to give him a private showing of the firm's best jewels at his hotel room. With the pick of the gems in his hand, he had slipped out of the hotel, leaving the hapless jeweler locked in the room. After mailing the haul to a Paris address, the phony Count rushed to the Croydon Aerodrome with his offer of £50 for the quick flight to France.

Mac and Charlie never saw the £50—only the bottles of champagne which the passenger could not consume in the short hop from Le Touquet to Paris. These they later consumed to drown their sorrow.

* * *

At least one KLM captain could have made a few shekels on the side if it had not been for a bit of female opposition! On one of his flights a passenger from the Near East entertained the erroneous idea that the captain was the lord and master of all he surveyed on the aircraft, which included the stewardess. Now the stewardess, being fair of face and figure, greatly appealed to the man. He wanted to buy her and offered the captain two camels and a sheep. When the captain gaped at him in astonishment, the Near Easterner thought perhaps the price was not high enough and generously added an extra three pigs.

After a detailed explanation of Western habits and rules, suffice it to say the dejected bidder was forced to return to the Near East without a reduction in his livestock inventory.

* * *

Back in the early days when scheduled air transport was still cutting its eye teeth on such aircraft as Fokkers, Ford tri-motors, Keystones and the like, airline pilots had some of their zaniest experiences. Some of these undoubtedly contributed to the fallacy that all pilots were a bit batty. Sometimes directly responsible for some of the queer goings-on were the narrow doorways of the F-3 Fokkers. Take the incident which happened in 1922 to Captain L. Sillevis of the KLM Royal Dutch Airlines who had the round-trip run between Amsterdam and London.

As a safety measure, the airlines ruled that before crossing the English Channel, passengers had to be issued life jackets and given instructions on how to blow them up, but with the admonishment that they were to be blown up only *after* leaving the aircraft in the event of a forced landing.

On this particular day Captain Sillevis went through this regular instruction routine and, as usual, everyone seemed to understand what they were to do in case of emergency—at least Sillevis failed to note any blank expressions on the faces of his charges.

An early KLM Fokker F-III taken in early 1920's.

Interior of KLM Fokker F-111, used by Royal Dutch Airlines in 1921-22.

Passengers and freight ready for early 1920's KLM London-Amsterdam flight in Fokker F-3.

No matter how meticulous the instructions, there's always some passenger who will "blow" it. Just ask KLM-Royal Dutch Airlines Captain L. Sillevis, shown here.　　　(KLM Photo)

Now the usual altitude when crossing the channel at that time was about 1,000 feet although there were times when strong head winds aloft made it advisable to fly at even lower elevations since tangling with such winds could readily make Irish stew of any flight schedule. This was one of the days when the breezes aloft were anything but cooperative and forced Sillevis to make this crossing at extremely low altitude; in fact he was practically on the threshold of "Davey's Locker!" High winds aloft had pushed him down to a mere 300 feet above the channel whitecaps. Here, though, where there were no winds to cut down their speed, they managed to make it into Amsterdam's Schiphol Airport exactly on schedule.

According to the manifest, a passenger was to disembark at Schiphol, so after swinging his aircraft into position by the terminal, Sillevis noted the attendant approaching with the passenger steps. The steps were rolled into position beneath the plane's exit and, as is customary, the attendant then placed

Early KLM DC-2's and DC-3's at Amsterdam's Schiphol Airport.

himself at the foot to assist those getting off or on the aircraft.

After several minutes, Sillevis peered out of the window and noted the attendant had disappeared. He wondered what had happened to him and the passenger who was to get off. Glancing back through the control room door, Sillevis saw the attendant in the cabin amid some sort of commotion near the exit. Opening the door for a better view, Sillevis was jarred into petrified amazement.

The passenger who was to disembark was trying to do just that but it was clear he wasn't going to make it; at least not in his present status. His life jacket not only was still engulfing him in loving embrace but now it was fully *inflated*! Red-faced and puffing, the man was going through a series of contortions, not unlike a wrestler about to sit in his own lap, trying his best to squeeze through the narrow aperture, the door of which was too narrow to accommodate both him and his pompous midriff. The hapless one looked for all the world like an angry puffed-up pigeon!

It seems that, having noted the pilot flying at such low altitude, the passenger assumed that meant just one thing—an imminent ducking—and in panic he had excitedly prepared

KLM Fokker F-3 at London in 1920's.

himself for the worst. As it turned out, the worst had come. His one escape from "disaster" now was to reverse the usual procedure and DEflate the billowing pillow encasing his middle since only then could he make his exit from the plane!

* * *

The narrow doors of those early-day Fokkers also brought about this episode for KLM's Captain R. Hofstra whose route was Paris-Brussels-Antwerp-Rotterdam-Amsterdam-Bremen-Hamburg. Hofstra not only transported passengers but various items of cargo which, not surprisingly, frequently included shipments of Parisian hats.

One particular shipment of these Paris creations slated for Hamburg constituted headgear of immense size, with brims as large as runways! In fact, they looked more like flying saucers and probably were quire capable of flying as well. Since they were so huge it was impossible to get them through the door opening, the hats were packed in boxes and tied to the Fokker's undercarriage which was then not yet retractable.

Upon arriving at Hamburg, Captain Hofstra strode under the liner to see to it that the boxes would be removed and the hats promptly sent on their way to the retailers. To his great astonishment he discovered that not a box was attached to the undercarriage of the plane! Hofstra looked at his crew helplessly. Whatever had become of those hats? But there was little need for speculation. They all knew what had happened. The flying saucers had taken off and were, by now, probably in

31

Flying saucers are real and early KLM-Royal
Dutch Airlines Captain R. Hofstra proves it!
(KLM Photo)

outer space! Now there would be the devil to pay as the
manufacturer of the millinery would hold the airlines responsible for the loss of the head finery.

Dejectedly Hofstra took off the next day on the return trip.
He kept scanning the landscape hoping against hope that in
spite of his altitude he might be able to see those missing boxes. All of a sudden he did see something although it wasn't
boxes. These were strange red, green and blue spots on the
moors of Luneberg. Were they beds of flowers? He nosed the
ship down to get a better look. The next minute he let out a
yell! They were hats—great big ones! There was no doubt but
that here were their missing flying saucers. They had broken
out of the boxes upon hitting the ground and had scattered to
the four winds across the moors.

Hofstra made a quick decision. No hat was going to out-
smart him. Spiralling down, he made a three-point landing in
the middle of the heather, after which he hastily scampered

32

after the hats before they decided to again take off.

This time there was no difficulty in getting them aboard the plane. The drop to earth had completely changed the entire appearance of the chapeaux. Even Hofstra, who was no particular lover of hats, especially extreme Paris ones, looked sadly at the colorful mess he had picked up and was to deliver to Hamburg. Their market value now had suddenly dropped to masquerade trade!

Hofstra sighed as he made his way to the control room. It seemed that even after all of his heroic efforts, there would still be the devil to pay.

* * *

Also during the 1920s Captain J. Duimelaar of KLM's Amsterdam-Paris run was assigned to fly a most unusual passenger—a four-legged one. Now he had transported animals before as this particular Fokker's cabin was equipped for animal transport. This animal, however, was the biggest and most cantankerous of any he had had to fly. This was a bull that had boarded the plane at Amsterdam to travel to Paris in style.

The bull accepted calmly enough being securely tied in the cabin and the speed and roar of the engine accompanying the take-off didn't seem to phase him in the slightest. In fact, the lumbering beast appeared quite docile, for which Captain Duimelaar thanked his lucky stars. Maybe, thought Duimelaar, the animal, like some people, was just naturally airminded and loved zooming through cloudland.

It wasn't long, however, before the bull's sweet and calm disposition literally took off! He began to snort and soon the snorting was accented by stomping of the feet which attracted the attention of the man "up front." At first Duimelaar wasn't certain what had brought about the change in the animal but as the plane gained altitude, the stomping increased and with more fury. Now Duimelaar understood what the trouble was. The change in atmospheric pressure was affecting the bull's

According to KLM-Royal Dutch Airlines Captain J. Duimelaar, that one trip was a lot of bull! (KLM Photo)

ears. However, ear ache or no ear ache, Duimelaar had to gain at least a minimum safe altitude so there was nothing to do but "take the bull by the horns," ironically speaking, and reach for it.

Now he realized this would set not too well with the bull even if he could explain it to him, so it was no surprise to Duimelaar that the animal objected so strenuously with all fours that there were times Duimelaar was positive he heard the floor boards cracking. Duimelaar's innards began to jell with fear. At this rate the floor wasn't going to last much longer. There was only one thing he could do—pray. So it was that all the way from Amsterdam to Paris Duimelaar sat in humble supplication, asking Him to see that the floor of his Fokker would be stong enough to allow him to land in Paris without four legs protruding from the bottom as well as the landing gear.

Duimelaar's prayers must have been answered as the floor was strong enough. It was Duimelaar who was not.

In the end the whole episode was entered in the KLM logs as a "lot of bull!"

* * *

There were the many little incidents flight crews experienced which were provoking or amusing—frequently both, depending upon their sense of humor. Here are some with which Royal Dutch Airlines, KLM, personnel have had to contend.

In 1927 KLM operated a charter service from Amsterdam to Indonesia for the distinguished American, W. Van Lear Black, which was the first intercontinental charter flight service in the world. The plane used in this connection was a Fokker F-7A which was flown by Captain G. J. Geysendorffer. Because of his social and business status, Van Lear Black invariably was met at the airports by prominent personnages and this particular flight was no exception.

As they neared their destination, Geysendorffer caught a glimpse of their landing field which now looked more like a seaplane base than an airport. Apparently one of those sudden torrential rain squalls that frequently hit this part of the world had just preceded them. It was obvious, however, that the deluge had not dampened the spirits of the welcoming committee as already they were waving enthusiastically. As Geysendorffer glided down to the puddle-filled field, the greeters augmented their wild waving with shouts of welcome for Geysendorffer's distinguished passenger. Van Lear Black, seeing the mass hand-waving of this cheering section, became equally excited. In his haste to reciprocate the greeting and "do it up brown" (which in this instance was certainly the right color), he opened a window and leaned far forward to enthusiastically wigwag back. At that precise moment Geysendorffer taxied through one of the lake-sized puddles. What happened next probably was one of Van Lear Black's most embarrassing moments. A billow of dirty water,

35

The welcome was all wet—and mighty muddy to boot!—says KLM-Royal Dutch Airlines Captain G. J. Geysendorffer.   (KLM Photo)

seemingly all of the water on the field, smacked him full in the face initiating an arrival-with-a-splash amid the undampened ardor of an equally soaked welcoming party!

Needless to say, before Van Lear Black could meet the official reception committee, there was a slight delay— something about "saving face!"

* * *

Hauling strange or unusual cargo is by now an almost every-day occurence with the airlines. El Al Israel Airlines, for one, has, during its many years of existence, transported its share of this type of freight, some of which caused no little excitement, along with headaches, to which El Al captains, such as Captain Leo Gardner, can testify.

When El Al initiated its freight department, its first freight was mainly gift food parcels. Since most of the food was sausages, the operation became known as "The Flying Sausage."

36

In those early days Mr. Haim Meirovitch, the oldest in line of service in El Al's freight department, would travel to the airport, check and sign out the food parcels, then bring them back to a storeroom which El Al Freight shared with a radio shop in Tel Aviv.

As such freight was perishable, Meirovitch would often find himself in a taxi delivering these parcels to people at their homes. Sometimes unclaimed food would go to stores or be thrown away. Later it was decided, instead, to turn these unclaimed goodies over to the Lod canteen. So it was that one El Al employee in the canteen took a bite of sausage and nearly broke a tooth. Since proud native sausage makers were not usually prone to leave pieces of bone or other foreign material in their sausage, the employee decided to probe for the source of his dilemma. Upon slicing open the sausage, lo and behold!—a diamond clattered onto his plate! Though the El Al employee could find little comfort in his sore tooth, he could not help but reflect that some woe-begone Israeli sausage maker could find even less comfort in his now diamondless ring.

* * *

There was also the time when the company's Constellations began flying to Johannesburg to bring back gold bullion and gold dust which, in turn, was trans-shipped to London. These shipments would arrive under heavy guard in the wee hours of the morning. One day the entire airport was in an uproar. A box of gold was missing! Since this could well result in a welter of woe for all concerned, terminating in serious consequences for a still phantom culprit, fever mounted to a high pitch before it was discovered that no one had absconded with the gold. All were in their proper place. Someone had simply miscalculated, triggering an uproar that more closely resembled a stirred-up ant hill than an orderly airport.

* * *

Lockheed "Constellation" operated by EL AL Israel Airlines for several years. Early EL AL hostess waving.

Hauling livestock also often resulted in unpredictable situations. Take the episode of the sacred Indian cows El Al was called upon to transport to Paris a few years ago. The cows and their Indian keepers were originally ticketed via another airline to Cologne where said "holy " cows were to be delivered to that city's zoo. At Frankfort Airport, however, they were stopped because of some local veterinarian violation and there they spent a miserable week of waiting. After the week, the authorities stated that either the cows would have to be moved or destroyed. In lieu of having them destroyed, Paris zoo officials said they were willing to accept the cows so they were shipped out on the next flight which happened to be an El Al Boeing. When the cows arrived at Paris in their highly "perfumed" state, the fire brigade had to be called out to not only hose off the week's filth from the bovines but from their keepers as well, after which one El Al Boeing underwent a thorough de-scenting.

* * *

38

Another Lod Airport upset was caused by a canine. The dog was brought in on a Constellation from England from whence he was following his much-travelled master who was in Israel for a short stay. The dog had received good treatment on the aircraft but nevertheless became disgruntled about something and managed to escape from his crate while it was being unloaded at Lod Airport. Seemingly the entire airport ran after the hound which sped down one runway after another at take-off speed. No one was swift enough to catch him and naturally this whole dog-gone business had the airlines' personnel in a tizzy, to say nothing of the dog's master who subsequently received the unhappy tidings.

Two days and many telegrams later, the cringing dog was found in a small village not far from the airport.

By that time the dog's master had returned to England so his pet was shipped off to meet him at the London airport. But next day, lo and behold, back came the dog on another El Al aircraft! The London airport had unceremoniously returned him because he had not been in quarantine; in fact, they wouldn't even let him get off the plane!

El Al personnel spent the next few days preparing the dog so they could send him back to London legitimately and this time, fortunately, he stayed.

* * *

This wasn't the first time El Al had experience with that type of passenger. A rather amazing incident at Lod Airport occurred during El Al's early Constellation days. The station manager at the airport occasionally found time to perform extra duties, such as the humanitarian gesture of taking any dog passenger for a short walk on the runway while the plane was refueling.

It so happened that one day the aircraft came in a little early and the station manager rushed out of his office to meet it without first checking the mail on his desk.

In the cargo hold he noted a large dog resembling a rather

shabby Alsatian. The dog looked at him with pleading eyes, clearly a mute supplication for release which a wagging tail confirmed. The kindly manager was only too willing to oblige but the dog was without a leash. Since ingenuity was then the order of the day, the man took a short length of rope, tied it around the dog's neck and patted him lovingly. The canine by now was wiggling from prop to rudder and emitting soft throaty sounds in eager anticipation.

Upon being led out on the runway the dog happily made exploratory runs, bounding and sniffing about in sheer glee. Everything was going along nicely although at times the manager was hard put to keeping up with this unusually frisky animal.

A few minutes later the dog willingly reboarded the airliner where, after some farewell pats, the manager put him back in his cage.

After the airliner took off, the manager went back to his office to check his mail. There on his desk was an urgent cable. It read: "Please be advised that a wolf, bound for the London zoo, is on board the plane. *Handle with extreme caution.*"

* * *

Problem passengers, however, are nothing new to El Al. Formed in 1948, El Al's early role was the transportation of immigrants from all over the world to Israel. In the early 1950s, in fact, entire populations were flown from Iraq, Yemen and other mid-East countries. To say the least, these flights were hazardous and the near-primitive passengers, most of whom had never seen an aircraft, much less flown in them, did nothing to help the situation.

The events of one such flight have been permanently etched into the memory of one early El Al crew.

This particular flight with a load of Yemen immigrants was Israel bound on one of those scorching days for which the mid-East is so well-known. Altitude did little to temper the oppressive heat.

40

El Al DC-4, hardly a place for an aerial bonfire, tea or not!

Suddenly the cabin door of the DC-4 opened and cups of hot tea were passed to a grateful and thirsty crew. Since El Al carried no hostesses in its early days, the first thought of the crew was, "What a noble gesture on the part of the passengers!"

Then came the second thought: "But where in the name of Solomon did the hot tea come from?"—a most logical thought considering there was no provision aboard for heating food or beverages, and Arabs knew nothing of thermos jugs.

As this second thought registered with impact, Radio Operator Joseph Swery was already on his feet and out into the cabin in one grand leap.

Sure enough! There, in the middle of the cabin, were their Arab passengers having a ball around a *bonfire*!

Snatching the handy tea urn, Swery was able to extinguish the fire before the ball became a blast.

Reprimanded, the passengers looked more than a little hurt. They had been told by the crew when boarding that there was to be absolutely no smoking. This order was obeyed to the letter but, obviously, the crew had failed to include bonfires in the edict!

* * *

41

How one flight in the C-47 (below) comprised
thousands of short hops is explained by Sabena
Captain F. Jenart (above).   (Sabena Photo)

A Sabena Airlines Douglas C-47 cargo airliner.

belgian world airlines

Here was another great flight—at least for the "passengers" as they literally were jumping for joy. The pilots, however, were not.

A Sabena freighter flight, scheduled to leave Brussels at night for Paris, had to be postponed to the next morning due to extremely strong crosswinds. Captain F. Jenart therefore was instructed not to come that night.

"The next morning," stated Captain Jenart, "I was surprised to learn while signing the loadsheet that I had to board via the small front door of the C-47 aircraft. When I asked the reason for this devious means of entry, the loadmaster replied it was due to the fact that the load consisted of an evenly disposed one-layer of uncovered boxes which occupied the entire floor of the main cabin. He went on to furnish the information that the plane had been loaded the prior evening and that the boxes contained small live frogs destined for Paris where they would be raised until their legs attained a size suitable to appease the appetites of the most meticulous of Parisian frog leg connoisseurs, at which time they would then be featured by one or more of Gay Paree's finer restaurants.

"Unfortunately, the loadmaster continued, during the night all of the frogs had "jumped jail" and were currently hopping pell-mell about the cabin.

"In the circumstances," said Jenart, "I decided not to investigate, but just leave well enough alone and let the little hoppers enjoy some liberty before their final trip to Paris and its frog leg gourmets.

"The flight happened to be a rather rough one, with considerable turbulence, and we discovered too late that due to those conditions, the door from cockpit to cabin could not be maintained locked. We also discovered that my 5,000 pounds worth of limping and jumping frogs, or about 20,000 of the critters, had a definite and curious propensity to invade the cockpit.

"My co-pilot spent more than an hour trying to hold that crowding mass of jumping legs with an assiduity that cost him his breakfast after the landing.

"The approach was also a jumping and limping one as it turned out that some frogs actually had succeeded in setting a straight course to the rudder pedals so that I could not ease my ILS approach, especially when from time to time I could feel those cold-blooded little devils trying to explore my trouser legs.

"At last we landed and I informed the dispatch they not only had to be careful when opening the rear door but that they had to collect their freight even in the cockpit—a chore in which they were not completely successful as for the next two weeks each crew reported finding one or two illicit "passengers" which were usually hidden in the vicinity of the rudder pedals.

"At least it no longer constituted a problem except for two

"Now, how could a sparrow board one of our ships without a ticket?" asks Captain Jack Winfield of New Zealand National Airways. Probably by putting it on his bill!   (NZNAC Photo)

minor things for the co-pilot and me. First, the next morning a Paris newspaper ran the story on its front page with the headline: 'PILOTS HAVE DIFFICULTIES ON LANDING,' underlined with: 'HIS FEMALE PASSENGERS WERE JUMPING IN HIS LAP.' And for the second, we—the co-pilot and I—for some time had a definite aversion for that famous dish known as 'frog legs'."

* * *

You undoubtedly have heard people in the "I'd rather keep one foot on the ground" category say that "flying is for the birds." Well, New Zealand National Airways not only has heard this remark but can prove that at least on one occasion there was some truth to the statement.

That one occasion occurred at Christchurch while loading a Viscount flight for Wellington. During loading operations an unticketed passenger somehow sneaked aboard and was not detected until after take-off when the hitchhiker—a sparrow—began flying up and down the cabin. The futile attempts by the stewardesses to apphrehend the culprit brought howls of glee from the passengers.

45

New Zealand National Airways Vickers "Viscount".

Finally the little stowaway simply vanished, probably because pressurization had taken effect or that it had just tired of the hide-and-seek game with the stewardesses. In any event, it remained quietly hidden until they landed in Wellington. However, when the door opened, the first to deplane was the feathered passenger! And the stewardess swore it emitted a "goodbye" chirp as it swooped past them into the "Wild Blue Yonder!"

Wellington sparrow population: up one!

* * *

Apparently nothing in the comic side ever happens on staid Air Bahama, but according to an Air Bahama captain, some of the line's far-ranging employees discovered this is not the case on other carriers.

Chief Pilot Everett W. Terry of Air Bahama passed on to us the following tidbit about an incident which happened to one

46

INTERNATIONAL
AIR BAHAMA

of Air Bahama's Miami reservations agents, Richard Streber.

It was a clear, bright and sunny day and Streber was enjoying a flight from Rochester to Chicago.

Seated next to him was a not-so-young lady, presumably tipping around 80, who also seemed to be enjoying the flight.

Streber eventually became involved in a political article in Time magazine when all of a sudden the little old lady next to him shattered his concentration with:

"Sonny, would you show me how to open my window? That cigarette smoke is really bugging me!"

* * *

Although venturing on a safari has afforded many travelers the excitement of their lives, perhaps the most unusual one was experienced by Captain Jose Romero Ruiz of Iberia Air Lines of Spain on what could rightly be called an aerial safari. The incident occurred on one of Iberia's flights from Bogota to Madrid, on the sector between San Juan and Madrid in 1964. Captain Ruiz, who was piloting the DC-8, gave us the following account:

"The purser, Mr. Cots, breathlessly burst into the cockpit and announced: 'Captain, a tiger is loose among the passengers!'

"I answered, 'Cots, leave the cockpit for a minute—calm down and tell it to me all over again.'

"Cots replied excitedly, 'It's true—it's true! There's a tiger cub loose in the tourist class aisle!'

An Iberia Airlines DC-8/52.

"As I followed Cots into the cabin, sure enough there was the tiger, looking rather wild-eyed at the confusion he had caused. By now a dozing passenger, disburbed by all of the excitement, opened his eyes and upon seeing the animal, yelled, '*Tiger!*'

"This outcry sent the cat scurrying under a seat from whence it disappeared under another seat and, in turn, it immediately disappeared under still another seat. It was clear that rounding up this agile cat wasn't going to be easy.

"A chase was organized, whereupon an Italian passenger traveling from Caracas to Rome via Madrid said: 'I'll take care of the tiger. This is my specialty; I'm accustomed to handling jungle animals!'

"Dropping on all fours, he began stalking the tiger while the less brave passengers retreated to safer quarters.

"Shortly thereafter the Italian captured and subdued his quarry. The only consequence of the chase was when the man, apparently feeling a rapport with the cat, extended an arm for an affectionate grasp of its neck and the tiger reciprocated the friendly gesture by extending its paws but neglecting to withdraw its claws.

"Some time after the excitement of the capture abated and everything was again under control, another passenger appeared and claimed the young tiger. The man had been hesitant to admit until now that he was responsible for all of this hubbub. The cat was being shipped by the University of Bogota to that of Madrid, and he had offered to take the animal in a heavy bag. Fearing it might suffocate, he opened the bag and with a true tiger's leap, the cat regained its temporary freedom.

"The Italian was congratulated all around for his bravery in capturing the tiger and in Madrid he was treated by a doctor who diagnosed the scratch on his hand as harmless."

* * *

As a rule most airline passengers prefer the comfort of their seats during flight, but according to El Al Captain Sam Lewis this certainly is not the case with El Al. Its passengers seem to have a strange habit in common—walking in air! It can actually be said that some literally walk to their destinations. Even meals cannot tempt these meandering Israelites to their respective seats, nor can the "Fasten Your Seat Belt" sign. They know El Al is their airline and, as such, it is "home" to them. On other lines they are obligated to maintain company manners in order to make the best impression, but on El Al that obligation is left behind.

This relaxed "at home" attitude extends from cross-aisle seat-to-seat hopping, length of the cabin visiting and in-the-aisle prayers.

A shining example of this is an incident reported by a non-national El Al passenger, an American attorney hailing from Providence, who was en route to Israel with a group of friends. Upon boarding at New York, the attorney found himself seated next to a priest. They had been airbourne but a few minutes when he noticed the priest's eyes literally popping out in surprise.

"What is *this*?" asked the amazed priest. He was referring

**El Al Captain Sam Lewis. He made Paris air-
port a daven-port!   (El Al Photo)**

to a commotion that had started and which had all the
resemblance of pandemonium in an airport terminal building.
People were up and pushing about and seemingly determined
to walk the entire distance to the Promised Land! This
pushing, milling about and jabbering continued for what seemed hours.

As the plane approached Paris, a rabbi told the attorney
that they would daven (pray) at the Paris airport. In short,
Paris airport would in all likelihood become a daven-port! A
few minutes later, however, in keeping with the situation on
board, they changed their minds. They would daven in the
back of the plane.

The rabbi therefore led 25 or 30 men, along with the
cooperative lawyer, to the tail of the ship where they proceeded to pray. Suddenly the plane hit a turbulent area and the
pilot urgently requested the passengers, who were now being
jounced around, to immediately sit down and fasten their seat
belts.

50

Since these people were devout daveners, stated the attorney, they didn't pay a bit of attention to the pilot. Who was *he* anyway?

The plane continued to rock back and forth and some suspected the pilot was doing it on purpose to make them sit down. This made them all the more determined to stay put and continue davening. If the truth were known, between the turbulence and the stubborn passengers in the tail section of the ship, the captain, himself, was about to daven! As the plane kept jouncing around, the attorney decided to leave the others to daven in the rear of the ship. He'd finish his prayers at his seat.

At the conclusion of his prayers at his seat, he noticed the priest reading his missal (book containing all the prayers and rites used by a priest in celebrating the Mass) and commented, "I guess we've gone about as far as ecumenism can go."

* * *

Former TWA Captain John A. (Johnnie) Guglielmetti has the feeling that his story should be in a book entitled "THE CAPTAIN HAD BETTER NOT SPEAK!"

The events that led up to this conclusion are as follows:

In 1928, after two years of flying the night airmail for Pacific Air Transport between Los Angeles and San Francisco, Guglielmetti became so enamored by the beautiful new Ford tri-motors owned by Maddux Airlines, a forerunner of Trans World Airlines, that he quit his mail job and signed on as Maddux's fourth-hired pilot. Maddux was then operating the first tri-motored passenger service between Tijuana and San Francisco via San Diego and Los Angeles.

Guglielmetti's job was rather routine until one day orders were received for him and his co-pilot, Louie Pratt, to proceed to San Diego, clear through customs and continue to Ensenada, Mexico, where a group of Mexican officials were waiting to be flown to Agua Caliente.

As their "Tin Goose," as the Ford tri-motors were affec-

1928 photo of then Maddux Air Lines Captain John A. Guglielmetti who tangled (almost) with the president of Mexico, and one of the Ford tri-motored airliners he flew. Guglielmetti later became a TWA captain.

tionately known, was circling Ensenada preparatory to landing, they noticed a group of people waiting on the field below. Upon landing and taxiing toward this group, it was further noted they were soldiers with rifles. These soldiers immediately surrounded the plane as it came to a stop. Guglielmetti's first thought was "We're prisoners!" and his lack of Spanish coupled with their lack of English did nothing to clarify the situation.

A short time later several cars containing civilians approached the plane. Anticipating an on-time departure, Guglielmetti had the engines running and his co-pilot was standing at the door. As the first passenger started to board the plane, Guglielmetti noticed that he and the others had six-shooters and were leaving them behind. Thinking they may be under the impression they could not bring their guns aboard, Guglielmetti left the cockpit and mentioned to the apparent

Maddux Airlines Ford tri-motor at Los Angeles.

leader of the group that it would be quite okay to bring their guns with them—a far cry from today's rules.

"You take care of your job up front, Capitan, and we'll take care of everything back here," was the surly reply.

Since this guy had kept his gun and sat in the last seat near the door, Guglielmetti decided he'd follow his advice and return to the cockpit. Then he began to wonder who this group was, and also whether their flight plans might be changed by them. At any rate, when all were aboard and the door slammed shut, Guglielmetti taxied out, took off and headed for Agua Caliente.

Everything was going smoothly until about midway in the flight. Suddenly a loud "bang!" was heard. Both Guglielmetti and co-pilot Pratt swung around in their seats to see who was shot or, worse yet, if *they* were being shot at. Everything seemed in order, all passengers dead-panning out of the windows as though nothing had happened. It was then that Pratt called Guglielmetti's attention to the right side of the landing gear. The tire had blown out with such force it had bent the wheel fender up. Now, although a blown tire on a Ford tri-motor loaded with passengers was not a matter to be taken too lightly, Guglielmetti was intensely relieved that they were not targets, or that an on-board assassination had not been carried

out. Guglielmetti had already decided, however, that if things got out of hand he would quickly restore order by throwing in a few stunts—for free!

Arriving at Ague Caliente and landing without incident despite the blown tire, their bandito-ish passengers were met by a group of people in cars and were last seen disappearing, without comment, down the road in a cloud of dust.

Although Guglielmetti and Pratt were not officially informed, unofficially they did hear that the leader of this group, and the one who had told Guglielmetti in no uncertain terms to go up and mind his own business, was none other than the then distinguished president of Mexico!

* * *

Even men of the cloth are not immune from the attentions of problem passengers.

Evangelist Billy Graham was on a trip from New York to Charlotte, N.C. On the same flight was a huge, obnoxious drunk, the fattest man Dr. Graham had ever seen on a plane. They had to take out the middle partition to give him two seats. He flirted outrageously with the stewardess and used the most obscene language imaginable.

After this had continued for some time, Mayor John Belk of Charlotte, also aboard the flight, turned to the drunk and asked him if he knew who was seated behind him. He replied that he did not and, accordingly, was informed by the mayor that it was none other than the Reverend Billy Graham.

Upon receiving this astounding information, the man, stumbling and swearing, got up and staggered back to where Dr. Graham was seated.

"Are you Billy Graham?" he asked.

Dr. Graham assured him he was, at which the obese imbiber held out his hand and loudly proclaimed:

"Well, put 'er there! Your sermons have sure helped me!"

* * *

What captain would enjoy the prospect of landing in the cold Aleutian Islands with a load of 108 potential trouble-makers destined for an island 318 howling, wintery miles farther on, every inch of it across the infamous Bering Sea? Not many, we would dare wager, yet that is precisely the lot which befell Captain "Pat" Baker of Reeve Aleutian a few years back.

Aleutian Flight 3 consisted of one Douglas DC-3, First Officer Hank Orth, the aforementioned Captain Baker and a cargo that included three crates of shivering, half-starved baby chicks, 36 per crate, 108 in all, en route from Seattle to St. Paul Island in the Pribilofs.

It was there at Cold Bay that the first inkling of trouble began. Problem number one was the weather report from St. Paul Island: "100 obscured, visibility one-fourth mile in fog, wind blowing 20 miles an hour and gusting to 40 straight across the runway."

Being early spring it was the time of year in that section of the world when strong, gusty winds give way to equally hazardous summer fog. Unfortunately this turned out to be one of those times that neither would yield to the other, so there sat Flight 3 cursed with both wind and fog, rare elsewhere but not too unusual out on the "chain," as the Aleutians are known northwise. In fact a 1949 weather report from Shemya read: "Ceiling zero, visibility zero, dense fog, wind 120° at 140 m.p.h., quonset huts blowing about on the runway." It really happened.

Problem two arose from a warning pasted to each crate of chicks—perforated cardboard containers measuring about 24" x 24" x 5"—advising that the chicks were not to be fed or

Captain Pat Baker

watered for 36 hours. Problem three was that, although the shipment originated in Seattle, no one seemed to know just when.

By this time it had become bitterly cold and had started to snow and blow—not an unlikely day at Cold Bay, the place simply living up to its name. Obviously, however, their feathered charges weren't up to surviving the night—and, as it turned out, the next two days and nights—in an unheated DC-3 so First Officer Orth commandeered an old Air Force warm-up hut located on the flight line, and there deposited the chicks. After plugging all the holes and cracks in the hut and firing up an ancient oil stove, Orth proceeded to the Air Force mess hall to scrounge feed for his fluffy friends. Upon the advice of the Mess Sergeant, Orth settled on some uncooked oatmeal as the best available chick chow. This, together with a quantity of pie pans in which to hold the oatmeal and a supply of water, turned the chick trick. They laid into the chow as though it were the Last Supper—which it was, almost.

The meaning of the warnings posted on each crate were clearly evident the following morning when it was discovered

Reeve Aleutian DC-3 at Cold Bay, Aleutian Islands.

Reeve Aleutian Airways DC-3 "loading up" at Cold Bay.

57

that, overnight, they had doubled in size! About this time Karl Kenyon, a U.S. Fish and Wildlife biologist traveling as a passenger to St. Paul Island to prepare the bureau's St. Paul lab for the arrival of fur seals, came by and said, "You guys are going to kill those chicks unless you find some sand for them. Without something like that they can't digest their food." Orth again raced to the rescue and with a trenching tool and an old bucket managed to find enough sand to save the chicks.

Three days later everything came up roses—weather-wise, that is—but definitely not chick-wise! By now the chicks had grown so big they couldn't be crammed into the original three crates with the aid of a pile driver. So back to the mess hall and another conference with the good ol' Mess Sergeant. Once again the M.S. came to the rescue with a supply of empty egg crates. Into these the 107 remaining "passengers" were crammed, one having gone to that big chicken house in the sky.

It took seven large egg crates to accommodate the chicks that three days earlier had arrived in three much smaller crates, and by the time they arrived at St. Paul, they were large enough to eat!

In spite of their problems with the chicks - turned chickens, the Reeve Aleutian crew thanked their lucky stars that their cargo wasn't rabbits!

* * *

Off-Beat

In this busy—or, perhaps, dizzy—business of air travel one would surmise that every phase of its operations would be geared to operate with the smoothness of silk. But, again, all is not gold that glitters, and where human element is involved, no matter how adept, boners or other off-beat incidents are bound to crop up to spark an otherwise run-of-the-mill day.

It would not be out of line, then, to tell about the unscheduled take-off of a West Coast Airlines captain, the details of which were related by Captain Patrick E. O'Grady, a senior captain of the airline which has since been taken over by Hughes Airwest.

The incident happened during the late 1950s when the DC-3 was still the standard aircraft for the local service air carriers such as West Coast Airlines. Several of the outlying stops were overnight stops and involved both aircraft and crew

"So the passengers and stewardesses didn't get on! At least we got off on time!" That's what Captain Patrick O'Grady of West Coast Airlines (now Hughes Airwest) seems to be saying in above photo. (Hughes Stratford Photo)

remaining from 10 to 24 hours. One of the responsibilities of the flight crew, besides completing a flight plan involving route, altitudes, time and fuel consumption, was to pre-flight the aircraft, and warm-up and check the engines at all such stops where a mechanic was not stationed. This was accomplished by starting the engines and taxiing to a warm-up area, checking the engines, and returning to the passenger terminal area for loading of cargo and passengers. North Bend, Oregon, was a station such as described and involved the aircraft and crew arriving in the evening and departing in the early morning of the next day.

West Coast Airlines had recently issued a directive to dress up the appearance of the operation. One of the stipulations was that the military hand salute would be the signal to the captain that all was clear for taxiing as far as the ground personnel were concerned. The return of the hand salute by the captain indicated that he was prepared for take-off. The aircraft was not to move away from the loading gate until the salute was given by the station person in charge.

West Coast DC-3.

On this particular day, the morning weather was marginal and threatened to become worse, possibly below take-off minimum. Some haste therefore was necessary to expedite the trip departure in order to get off at least one step ahead of the weather. The captain and first officer hurried out to the DC-3 to complete the warm-up. The station personnel removed the rudder, elevator and aileron blocks but did not remove the landing gear pins as only a warm-up was indicated. A fire guard was posted for the start of each engine and after they were running, the station manager unthinkingly saluted the captain merely as a friendly gesture. This hand gesture and its return salute by the captain immediately started a chain of action in the crew's mind. With the threatening weather and the need for expediting the trip departure, the captain and first officer naturally assumed the passengers had already been boarded and warm-up was to be accomplished at the end of the runway, therefore they immediately taxied there.

In the meantime, the station manager returned to the station to complete ticketing the passengers but the next thing both he and the passengers observed was the DC-3 taking off! The thoroughly perplexed station manager, wondering what in thunder was going on, rushed to the company radio in time to hear the captain had a complaint—the landing gear wouldn't retract! Well, *that* part of this unexpected fiasco certainly was no surprise to the ground crew. The station manager acknowledged the captain's comment by transmitting to him the stunning information that there was good reason the landing gear was so uncooperative. The landing gear pins were still in; not only that, he had left both the passengers and stewardess behind!

There was a moment or two of definite silence, then, in a rather subdued tone of voice, came the captain's request for a return to the airport. This not only required a complete instrument let-down due to the weather but involved a complete air traffic control let-down clearance.

Twenty minutes later a very red-faced captain and first officer landed and taxied up to the gate to pick up the passengers and stewardess they had left behind.

* * *

Most lines, if not all of them, have at sometime or other inadvertently misdirected a passenger's luggage, or sold the same seat to two people. There even have been occasions when things got a bit mixed up in air cargo. In this latter connection a captain of New Zealand National Airways Corporation cites the following.

Among the more frequent users of NAC's air freight service are New Zealand's many racing clubs. Cannisters of horse swabs addressed to the New Zealand Racing Conference are a familiar sight at the Wellington Freight Depot.

"If the horse piddle freight is on board—let's go!" New Zealand National Airways Captains Bob Anderson and Bill Pattie.

(Hamilton, N.Z., Times Photo)

One day an NAC clerk attended a man at the counter who, in a broad English county accent, requested, "The horse piddle freight, please." The clerk, proud of his unerring comprehension of accents of all kinds, unhesitatingly took this as a rather basic translation of the freight consignment to the Racing Conference and promptly handed over four shiny cannisters.

Off drove the recipient to Wellington Hospital where he happily handed the four cannisters over to the laboratory staff. Luckily, a staff member of the hospital had at one time also worked for the Racing Conference and immediately recognized the horse swabs. The four shiny cannisters, of course, were duly dispatched to their correct destination.

After this embarrassing mixup one very chagrined NAC clerk began exercising extreme caution whenever confronted with accents—broad or otherwise.

* * *

Pioneer airmail pilot and United Air Lines Captain E. Hamilton (Ham) Lee. "There ought to be an easier way to announce a war!"
(United Air Lines Photo)

Sometimes it doesn't pay to get up—up in the air, that is!

One of these occasions involved veteran United Air Lines Captain E. Hamilton Lee, better known in his element as just plain "Ham."

It was December 7, 1941, a date that supposedly was to have lived in infamy. For Ham Lee, it has—but not for the same reason President Roosevelt had intended it should. It all came about as Lee was cruising along in a fully loaded DC-3 Mainliner between Los Angeles and San Francisco and, under his breath, secretly cursing the demons that caused him to fly on instruments through thick clouds all the way.

Among other passengers, there were aboard two high-ranking officials of United Air Lines which, together with the clouds, already made two situations he could have well done without.

Having reached his assigned cruise altitude, Lee turned the controls over to his co-pilot and tuned the cockpit radio to a KFI news broadcast. Suddenly a special news bulletin flashed over the air: "The Japanese are at this moment bombing Pearl Harbor in Hawaii and Manila in the Philippines. Loss of lives and ships is heavy!"

Ham immediately left the cockpit and made his way through the passenger cabin to inform the UAL officials of what he had heard on the radio. To his amazement, his reception was nothing short of frigid. Not only did they not believe a word of what he had to say but they suggested that Lee might apply himself far better at the controls up front than rushing into the cabin with such asinine statements. With this total let-down, Lee dejectedly made his way back to the cockpit.

Nearing the little central California oil town of Coalinga about half way between Los Angeles and San Francisco, flying at 8,000 feet and still in the soup, there was a sudden terrific explosion and disintegration of the windshield.

Both Lee and his co-pilot were as sure as the good Lord made little green apples that the Japs had arrived over California and had them in their ring sights until they discovered blood, feathers and glass all over themselves and the cockpit. Upon mopping up, they managed to fathom that ducks were also on instruments at 8,000 feet! This indeed took their minds completely off the war, as what December flight wouldn't to a wet and shivering pilot and co-pilot zooming along at three miles a minute without a windshield in front of them!

From this experience Ham Lee learned not only that ducks also fly by instrument but that some days, for sure, it doesn't pay to get out of bed, to say nothing of off the ground.

* * *

Crews of KLM (Royal Dutch Airlines), too, have not been without their off-beat incidents. In fact many such gems are still rife in the memories of KLM flight personnel. One such incident took place on one KLM captain's Amsterdam-New York flight. Stewardess Kremer issued chewing gum to an elderly lady with the routine remark that it prevented buzzing in the ears during the take-off. She noticed later that the woman had plugged her ears with it.

* * *

Another KLM captain on an Amsterdam-South America flight tells about an incident that happened to Stewardess Klopper. Before the take-off she noticed that an aged woman looked rather nervous. Hoping to allay any fears the woman might have, the stewardess sat beside her and held her hand. When the notice "Fasten Seat Belts" went out, Miss Klopper got up to go on with her work, whereupon the woman said, "If you're frightened again, my dear, just come and hold my hand again!"

* * *

Still another KLM captain tells about this unusual happening on one of his Amsterdam-Basle runs, which turned out to be an honorable occasion for KLM few airlines can boast about.

Aboard the plane were some passengers from Stockholm, one of whom was an expectant father. During the flight a telegram arrived for him which announced, "Daughter born." The proud new father, so enthusiastic about KLM's super service, immediately chose the names Kasja Lena Marianna so that the child would have the initials KLM in honor of the airline. In addition, Miss Boon, the stewardess, later stood sponsor for KLM at the babe's christening in Stockholm. This is probably the only child in all creation with the Royal Dutch Airlines as its godparent!

* * *

Among many people these days there's a thing about smoking. Indulging in the use of tobacco has been pronounced harmful to one's health by the Surgeon General of the United

There ought to be enough room for cigar smoke in a Braniff Boeing 747!

States; therefore many have—in the vernacular—kicked the weed and any number of non-smokers have decided to remain just that: non-smokers in the interests of good health and stamina.

One anti-smoker in the pilot ranks of Braniff International has such a hang-up about physical fitness that he allows no smoking in the ranks of his crew members and permits no passenger in the cabin to smoke cigars.

On a non-stop 747 cruise to Honolulu, the captain detected cigar smoke. He immediately summoned the hostess, one of 15 years' service with a personality passengers loved and who could be plain-spoken when the occasion warranted, and this seemed to be one of those warranted occasions.

Captain: "Is there someone smoking in the cabin? You know I don't permit cigars on my ship."

Hostess: "Yes, sir. A gent in first-class is enjoying his cigar with his after-dinner liqueur and bothering nobody."

Captain: "You go back and tell him to put it out!"

Hostess: "Sir, if you want it put out, *you* go back and tell him yourself!"

Captain: "You *know* I can't leave this cockpit except for physiological reasons."

Hostess: "Then why don't you go back there and douse his cigar and kill two birds with one *physiological* call?"

Thereupon one subdued BI captain continued on to Hawaii with mixed emotions, i.e.: emotions fraught with cigar smoke and hostess sass.

* * *

It is the opinion of some pilots that United Air Lines pilots are somewhat uppity and, whether true or not, consequently become piqued with this supposed attitude. This was indicated quite clearly one day when a United Air Lines crew came in for a bit of ribbing administered by a Braniff International crew.

It happened at Des Moines when Captain Jack Mason and First Officer Pendarvis, taxiing out in a Braniff One-Eleven, found themselves almost parallel with the UAL 727 about the same time, as both flights waited for clearance from the tower.

Tower: "Okay, who is going to be the gentleman this morning and give way to the other?"

BI's pilot picked up the mike and, with tongue-in-cheek, said, "Okay, Braniff, go ahead!"

As the Braniff plane taxied in front of the UAL cockpit, the UAL crew, natch, was glaring—eyeball to eyeball.

* * *

What happens when a pilot sees a sight so astoundingly beautiful that he can't bear to look at it?

Like a script from "One Step Beyond," this is precisely what happened to United Air Lines Captain Larry Peyton. The date was May 18, 1934, and, although forty years ago, Peyton recalls it as though it were but yesterday.

Then a co-pilot, Peyton was teamed with Captain Grant Anderson flying United's Flight 4 from San Francisco to Salt Lake City. It was one of those crystal clear late spring nights with which the high western desert country is occasionally blessed. The sky was nothing short of magnificent. Its stars looked for all the world like sparkling diamonds; its planets like beacons, and the Milky Way a breathtakingly brilliant carpet of light across the dome of the sky from horizon to horizon. There was no moon, which served the dual purpose of accentuating the stars in all their splendor and bathing all below in Stygian blackness, except for the faint outline of ridges and mountain peaks. The sweeps of airways beacons, rotating along their path of flight, brushed the ground with fingers of silver.

As Flight 4 approached Elko, Nevada, Captain Anderson, tired of flying and needing a rest break, turned the controls over to Co-pilot Peyton and went aft to stretch his legs. Alone in the cockpit, Peyton turned off the instrument lights to better enjoy the starlit sky.

Upon clearing Secret Pass, Peyton began a gradual letdown for Salt Lake City. Over Little Lake Pass at 10,000—south of Wendover at 8,000 and out over Bonneville salt flats at approximately 3,500 feet.

It so happened that Bonneville flats was completely flooded that year, causing it to resemble a mammoth lake, and on that particular night the water was as smooth as glass. As Peyton flew out over the mirror-like surface, it picked up the star-studded sky in flawless reflection and created what Peyton later described as "the loveliest sight I have ever beheld. There were stars above, stars below, stars all around me. Everything, everywhere, ablaze with stellar beauty!"

Completely enchanted, Peyton sat back and drank in the beauteous spectacle, allowing his eyes to rove so as not to miss a particle of it.

All of a sudden it hit him—VERTIGO! He was literally in another dimension, not being able to tell if he was rightside up, upside down, on his side, going straight up or coming straight down. He was completely disoriented— literally lost in those stars with no reference points; no way of telling what was

Braniff Airlines Boeing 727.

straight and level—or normal.

Fortunately at this point, Peyton's years of training took over. He quickly turned the instrument lights full on, tuned in the Salt Lake radio range and continued the flight on instruments, one of the almost non-existent occasions instrument flying was necessitated on a crystal clear night. Upon again assuring positive control, Peyton stole another glance outside which immediately resulted in another wave of vertigo. Thereafter he kept his eyes on his instruments until safely past Lake Bonneville and over the safety of familiar unreflecting dry land.

Peyton, in summing up the experience later, remarked that he was, both, completely delighted and awed by that exhilarating and frightening situation—delighted by its sheer splendor, and so awed that he couldn't stand it!

* * *

With the preceding episode being reminiscent of a sublime sight developing into a ridiculous situation, perhaps we should now conclude this chapter with a ridiculous situation devoid of any semblance of sublimity. It goes like this:

Vas is los here? (What's wrong here?)

Two airliners were single-filed at Chicago's O'Hare runway ready for take-off, one a German Lufthansa Boeing 707, the other a Braniff Boeing 727.

Said the Lufthansa pilot in thick German accent:

"O'Hare Tower, dis iss Lufthansa 500. Ve are ready for take-off."

Coincidentally, the Braniff 727, immediately behind, also had a German-born pilot.

"Dis is Braniff 142—ve are also ready for take-off."

There was a short pause and then this reproving remark from the Lufthansa mike:

"Dot's not funny, Braniff!"

* * *

PSA Boeing 727 always turns right at first ocean out of Los Angeles.

3

Communications—
SNAFU and Otherwise

The radio—or P.A. system—"mike" has always fascinated pilots one way or another. Either they like it or hate it. The gabby ones love it—one even going so far as singing to the passengers (see chapter six)— and those inclined to be taciturn detest the whole idea. Of course even the taciturn pilot becomes accustomed to his microphone duties but never elaborates—he just "gives the facts, ma'am!"—while the loquacious ones yak ever onward, the following being a perfect example of this repartee by a Pacific Southwest Airlines (PSA) captain Oakland-bound but still on the ground at L.A.:

"Ladies and gentlemen, this is your captain. I thought you'd like to know this is an airplane. Boeing built it. They call it a 727. Our company bought it. They call it Flight 243 to Oakland. We'll be taking off in a few minutes flying due west. Now we all know you can't reach Oakland by flying due west, so we're going to make a right turn at the first ocean we come to. This trip should take about 52 minutes if the co-pilot does his job right!"

* * *

Another line's captain soothed his charges with the following:

"Ladies and gentlemen," he began over the speakers, "this is your captain welcoming you aboard and hoping you have a most pleasant trip. We will fly at 12,000 feet. You may wonder why we are going to fly at 12,000 feet. Well, the reason we are going to fly at 12,000 feet is because we ain't going to fly any higher that 12,000 feet. And now we'll taxi out to the end of the runway and try to get this thing off the ground—on schedule!"

* * *

As another fair example, a Western Airlines captain, flying over Crater Lake in Oregon, entered into a lengthy P.A. system dissertation, explaining to his passengers the origin, depth, diameter, circumference, number of gallons and a myriad other statistics on the famous lake as they circled the area. At last they proceeded toward their destination. Shortly a note came to the captain from a passenger via the stewardess. It read:

"You forgot to tell us how long it would take to suck it through a straw!"

* * *

Verbose captains aside, it is a known fact that many otherwise boring flights are often sparked by inadvertent P.A. system booboos. One of the tall tales cropping up every so often concerns the airline captain who, tired from a long monotonous flight, said to his first officer, "What I need most now is some sex and a good, dry martini."

Unknown to the captain, his mike button was switched on at

the P.A. position and his presumably private conversation was heard by all aboard the plane.

The stewardess in the rear of the plane made a wild dash forward to tell the captain to turn off the P.A. system.

Half way up the aisle, a little old lady reached out, stopped the stewardess, and said:

"Oh, miss! You forgot the martini!"

* * *

Of course, the foregoing is exactly what we have dubbed it—a tall tale. It really didn't happen, but it well illustrates the confusion that can be caused should airline communications actually *become* snafu'd—be it P.A. systems, radio communications, cable or teletype—and you may be sure that, at times, they do just that. Following are a few actual situations:

Airline captains who hold a regular flight schedule on a particular route are often required to maintain proficiency over other airways. Often when you see an extra person deadheading in the cockpit with the uniformed crew, he's riding as an observer or "sidewalk superintendent" to maintain his personal qualifications for that route.

This day it was United Air Lines Captain Harlan A. Gurney's turn to brush up on the airway to Seattle. Daylight was doing a fast fade-out as their wheels parted company with San Francisco International Airport. Within the hour night had carressed the Trinity Alps and all that could be seen was the flash of the ship's navigation lights on the clouds. Gurney, noting several of the radio facilities had been altered, thought it best that he review his charts where he could see them better, so he walked back to the cabin.

Stopping at the buffet, he spoke to the stewardess in charge to let her know he wanted to review his maps in the lounge. She said her name was Dorene, and she was the kind of girl who made a captain wish he had much less seniority, not more; the sort of lass into whose pink ear he would like to whisper sweet somethings—or nothings, as would most likely be the case.

United Air Lines Captain Harlan A. (Bud) Gurney. There are times when seniority is an asset, and this was one of them.
(United Air Lines Photo)

As Dorene and Gurney finished their short conversation, the voice of the captain came through very clearly over the P.A. system. "Dorene, are you there?" he asked in tones soft as velvet. Obviously the wrong switch position had been selected and although the captain thought he was speaking only to Dorene, his words were being broadcast to all of the passengers who were now more than a little alert at the unbusiness-like voice. Men lifted appreciative eyes toward the pretty stewardess and women tilted their heads in anticipation. You could practically see their ears stretching upward and outward. Until then Gurney never had realized so many ears could resemble radio antennas, but suddenly his entire cabin was seemingly mass radio-ized. And now, considering the pulchritude involved and that "something" in the captain's voice, every ear was attuned to pick up the captain's message of love.

Late photo of now retired UAL Captain Bud
Gurney and wife, Hilda, beside their hobby— an
antique DeHaviland Moth.

Dorene tried to squelch the speakers but the captain's switch
controlled this demoniacal system. "Lenny," she said in
desperation, "you are on P.A. position!" Lenny, however,
went blithely on, his words getting in the way of his ears.

"You know what I want, Dorene, don't you? Can't you hear
me, darling?" asked he in dulcet tones.

Several men burst into loud guffaws and there were ill-
concealed giggles among some of the women, while others
grinned in high amusement. Dorene's cheeks turned a hot
scarlet and she prayed the voice would stop. But the words
went on with sugary sweetness although the giggling in the
cabin drowned out all but the last phrase:

" . . . and remember, two sugars and one cream."

Gurney went on back and read his charts in a very quiet
cabin.

* * *

Western Air Lines Captain Jerry Keeley at least tried to point out why Western Air Lines "is the ONLY way to fly!" (Davis/McIntyre Photo)

So it has been proven that it isn't always the novice who runs into embarrassing situations where communications systems are concerned. Coming in for his share of woes is also the seasoned operator who with equal dexterity can cope almost simultaneously with two speaking devices, namely the Public Address system and the Air Traffic Control (radio) system. There are times, however, when the rapidity of changing from one to the other, especially after several minutes of quick see-sawing between speakers, can put a pilot in a verbal "flat spin" from which he usually emerges with a face as red as a summer sunset.

Captain T. G. "Jerry" Keeley of Western Air Lines found himself in just such a predicament one day while captaining WAL's Flight 90 Fan Jet between San Francisco and Denver. He had turned the controls over to the co-pilot and taken charge of the radio on this leg of the flight. For some time he was busily engaged in talking to the A.T.C. (Air Traffic Control) controller in the tower which necessitated changing frequencies quite rapidly. They had just reached cruising altitude and were crossing over the High Sierras, eastbound, when Keeley, obviously one of the more talkative captains, having completed his conversation with A.T.C., decided it now would be an ideal time to give the passengers some in-flight information. This was a task Keeley usually turned over to the co-pilot or second officer but since he was commanding the radio end of things today, he thought he might as well also make the P.A. announcement.

Replacing the radio microphone, he picked up the P.A. speaker but at that moment another radio call came in from A.T.C. and Keeley quickly switched microphones. At the termination of his conversation with the tower, he proceeded with information to the passengers as to altitude, speed, weather conditions, time of arrival and points of interest. Divulging the latter bit of news took considerable time as Keeley went to great lengths in telling them of all the major and minor points of interest they should look for and which included practically every mountain, valley, river and hen roost en route. Upon completion of his oratory, he felt extremely pleased with himself as he was certain the now well-informed passengers would enjoy the trip to the fullest. As he leaned back, almost smugly, A.T.C. flashed on and a voice teasingly cooed: "It sounds like you are going to have a *real good* flight!"

Captain Keeley stared at the microphone in stunned amazement. "I *couldn't* have! flashed through his head. But he had! He had talked into the wrong microphone and so had wasted his entire flowery speech on A.T.C.!

Although it had deprived the passengers of the benefits of his efforts, it had provided the A.T.C. lads and Keeley's flight crew with one of the best laughs of the year, in which laughter Keeley, himself, also joined after he overcame his initial shock.

* * *

Frequently radio messages between flight crew and ground personnel are misunderstood due to static and other atmospheric disturbances. For instance, there was the conversation between Captain Richard P. "Dick" Craine, senior United Air Lines pilot, and Honolulu International somewhere over the Pacific between the mainland and Hawaii. In accordance with interstate regulations governing the entry of foreign or out-of-state plants, fruits and the like, into the islands, a spray insecticide bomb must be used prior to landing the aircraft. And so it was on this particular flight that Captain Craine was all set to fumigate his craft but made the sudden discovery that not a single insect bomb was aboard. Picking up his mike, he passed on the bad news that "We don't have a spray bomb aboard!"

He awaited the reply—almost certain the stern directive would be, "Then don't land here—take your bugs some place else!" Instead, for several seconds, there was utter silence at the other end.

The startled voice that finally boomed back practically shattered Craine's eardrums. It was clear the man wasn't only excited—he was on the verge of panic!

"Radio silence! Radio silence!" he shouted. "Plane with bomb on board please *come in*!"

After due explanation, Craine decided the next time he'd say "insect repellent" and thus prevent another complete tizzy at HNL.

Came the next time. But what happened? To Craine's "We don't have any 'insect repellent' aboard," came the query, "How do you spell that?"

Craine concluded that no matter how you phrase it, you can't win!

* * *

Speaking of snafu'd communications, here's one for the birds!

Western Airlines Captain Norm Edson, flying WAL Flight

80

Western Air Lines Captains Jim Conniry and Norm Edson come up with a "bird" of a story. (Davis/McIntyre Photo)

601 out of San Francisco, was informed that WAL Captain Jim Conniry was aboard deadheading to Los Angeles where he was scheduled to fly WAL Flight 466 that afternoon.

To accommodate his fellow pilot, Edson dispatched a message to Airinc at Los Angeles informing them to "advise Western dispatch that we have Conniry on 601 for flight 466 this afternoon."

Unfortunately, this was a verbal rather than a written message which accounts for the following acknowledgment:

"Roger, understand, advise Western dispatch you have canary on flight 601 for flight 466."

Detecting nothing amiss, Edson came back with, "That's right. He's captain for flight 466."

The puzzled airline operator, after sending the message, called Western dispatch and asked, "Did that teletype message about the canary make sense to you or was the captain just pulling my leg?"

It was enough to get everyone all a-twitter!

* * *

Frequently the co-pilot, or first officer, gives birth to humorous incidents. For instance, there was the co-pilot aboard an airliner which was icing up so rapidly that a crash landing seemed imminent. This was a situation to which the co-pilot had never been introduced and he certainly didn't relish shaking hands with it, so to speak. It also was a situation which called for the steadiest of nerves but already his innards would give a belly dancer keen competition. He wondered if the captain had graduated from such an internal state of affairs but one look at this partner's face told him he was at least outwardly worried even if he wasn't inwardly shook up. The situation, in any case, was serious.

Determined to do his bit in the crisis, the co-pilot's intellectual mechanism whirred with ways and means of saving their skins. Suddenly he recalled that in such precarious situations, the "company" should be kept notified, if at all possible. Turning to the ice-battling and perspiring captain, the eager beaver co-pilot, pleased that he had recalled this directive, anxiously inquired if it would be all right to transmit the distress signal which happens to be "May Day" in the radio-telephone vernacular. Realizing the seriousness of their plight, the captain instructed his flying mate to proceed with the message.

With that, the co-pilot nervously grabbed the mike with one damp hand and excitedly began yelling, "Maytag! Maytag! Maytag!"

* * *

The most embarrassing moment for a Braniff captain pulling out of Dallas en route to Chicago was when he picked up the P.A. mike as they winged out past the Sherman-Dennison area near Lake Texoma and announced to the passengers:

"Good morning, ladies and gentlemen. We are now passing over the shitty of Cerman, Texas on our left." (City of Sherman, Texas.)

Realizing his tongue twister, he burned with embarrassment

and retired into the comparative solitude of the cockpit. He hoped no one had noticed his blooper.

However when he arrived at Chicago, one passenger waited and approached the captain as he came out of the cockpit.

"Did you say what I thought you said?" the passenger asked with a chuckle.

"Yes, I did and my apologies," said the captain.

"I thought that was what you said, but nobody else laughed so I didn't either," said the passenger, "but your slip of the tongue made my trip today."

* * *

Years ago, before radar on airliners, one of the most perplexing problems of pilots was severe thunderstorms. Quite often they would get caught inside them and plane, crew and passengers alike would undergo a ride that would make the promenade deck of a bucking bronc seem tame in comparison.

One young United Air Lines captain, who as a co-pilot had taken several such rough rides, was particularly leary of these sky turmoils. On one of his first trips as a captain, he flew toward an area of threatening weather. Properly exercising due caution, he started a wide detour and was extending tender loving care to his passengers by asking them on the P.A. system to fasten their safety belts.

His announcement went like this: "Ladies and gentlemen, we are thunderingly approaching a line of rapid storms. Please safen your fasty belts!"

A KLM Fokker F-XVIII "Pelican".

Although the following cannot be classified as a snafu'd communique, one must put the proverbial two and two together to get the true meaning.

Captain Arthur Cheney reported that while a Western Airlines flight was taxiing up to the terminal, this announcement was made by the stewardess over the P.A. system as part of her arrival message:

"Will all passengers please check under their seat belts for their personal belongings."

The result of this announcement was a cabin full of laughing passengers and one badly flustered stewardess.

* * *

This little episode occurred in 1933 on one of Captain Smirnoff's Amsterdam-Djakarta runs for KLM Royal Dutch Airlines, which turned out to be a record flight from Europe to Asia. Smirnoff's co-pilot at the time was Piet Soer. In a telegram that was sent the name Soer was inadvertently changed to Soeur (French for "sister").

When Smirnoff brought the Fokker F-18 Pelican down for a short intermediate landing at Karachi, the press photographers dispatched to cover this record flight asked Smirnoff where his sister was!

* * *

In the wee 1930s, during United Air Lines pre-burgeoning period, one of the innovations of the day was, of course, airborne radio, and because company pilots acted like kids with a new toy when making their regular position reports over this new gadgetry, base stations could expect most anything from them—anything to spice up the day, that is.

Radio shenanigans by the pilots were especially rampant in the sparsely settled areas of the West. One of the wildest, most desolate of UAL's routes was that which lay between Cheyenne and Salt Lake City. We say "was" with tongue in cheek since it probably is still lying there beneath its blanket of sagebrush, prairie dogs and jackrabbits, though now far beneath the jet routes seven miles above. But since those were the days of what today would literally be considered "on deck" flying (anything lower would be "hedge hopping"), and since there was considerable distance between towns, pilots would make their regular 20-minute progress reports over whatever landmark met their eyes, and apparently their eyes beheld some pretty outlandish ones, not the least being Eads Ranch outhouse, Tie Siding and Jenkin's windmill.

Each pilot, for instance, was well aware that most of these landmarks were not indicated on the route maps in the base station radio rooms, and it became a "game" with them to report from a point they knew wasn't on the map, then land and show the base radio operator its location. These carryings-on soon resulted in the maps becoming a mish-mash of inked-in landmarks.

One UAL pilot reported in one night that he was "over Wyoming." Since he was flying between Rock Springs and Cheyenne, he obviously *had* to be over Wyoming. He was acknowledged by the base operator with, "O.K., but *where* over Wyoming? The answer was simply a repeat with no further explanation. Upon landing, however, the pilot showed the base operator a point on the map where there was nothing but an old railroad section house. On it was a sign which read "Wyoming!"

Another pilot radio'd in that he was *exactly* 86 miles east of Rock Springs.

"How do you *know* you're *exactly* 86 miles east of Rock Springs?" challenged the base operator at Cheyenne.

"Well, because there's a sign right off my left wing that says so, that's why!" was the answer.

It turned out that he had encountered a low overcast and had climbed through it only to find another overcast above. This soon lowered to meet the one below. His ship commenced accumulating a heavy load of ice and figuring discretion was the better part of valor, he decided to land. Feeling his way down through the overcast, he finally broke out fairly close to the ground. Picking a reasonably smooth spot next to a highway, he landed. Just as his ship came to the end of its landing roll, Cheyenne called for a position report. Looking up, lo and behold! there immediately off his left wing was a highway sign reading:

"Rock Springs—86 mi."

* * *

Not all of United's pilots were elated over this new-fangled radio equipment. One pilot in particular would check his equipment with the base station, report his time off the ground, and then completely ignore his regular 20-minute interval position reports. The next time he would be heard from was when he approached his next landing point, and all admonitions as to the importance of regular position reports each 20 minutes were to no avail. He'd simply say, "I just can't understand it—the radio just wouldn't work!" The equipment was checked and re-checked and nothing found, yet the whole rigamarole was repeated on the next leg of the flight.

Suspicioning what was taking place, the pilot was watched through high-powered field glasses. Suspicions confirmed! Sure enough, immediately upon take-off he would remove his radio headset and put on his cap!

The following episode finally cured our radio-shy hero:

He had taken off eastbound from Salt Lake for Cheyenne. After reporting his take-off time, the usual siege of radio silence set in and, but for the teletyped reports of his progress from caretakers at various emergency fields along the route, he could have been flying over Timbuktu.

All was fine, thanks to these TWX's from the caretakers, until he had passed Cherokee, Wyoming. He should have then been reported next over Medicine Bow. No report from that point but this was plausible since pilots often flew south of there straight through to Laramie. Likewise, no report from Laramie. Hmmm! Finally, when he had not arrived at Cheyenne when he should have, a search plane was readied.

Just as the search plane was ready for take-off, the base radio blared out:

"Plane 286 calling Cheyenne."

"Cheyenne calling 286. Where in blazes are you?"

Back came his reply: "I'm stuck in a badger hole!"

"O.K., 286, you're stuck in a badger hole but *where* is the badger hole?"

His answer was merely, "I'm stuck in a badger hole but I'll be in soon."

In about an hour, sure enough, in came our hero in 286. Upon landing he was immediately invited into the division superintendent's office where his story was, to put it mildly, anxiously awaited.

He had, as was surmised, cut south of Medicine Bow for Laramie. Cutting through a valley, he met a cloud bank head

United Airlines Boeing 40-B mail plane in 1928, the type ship that wound up in a badger hole.

on. Not being able to get under it and not wanting to try to fly over it, he turned around hoping to approach Laramie from another direction. However, in passing through the upper end of the valley, he had stirred the early morning air just enough to create fog in his wake and when he reversed his course, there it was—a fog bank staring him right in the face. At this point he decided he had better set down and wait for the fog to burn off.

He landed in an open meadow and had just about stopped rolling when, plunk! down went one wheel in a badger hole. Too deep in the hole to blast the wheel out with his engine, there was naught to do but get out and dig. Checking his tools, all he could find was a screwdriver. This proved about as effective in getting his Boeing out of a badger hole as trying to put out a fire with an eyedropper. A piece of wood, found nearby, was equally useless. Noticing a small shack about a half mile distant, he hiked over and, luckily, found an old shovel. With this he was able to dig around the wheel enough so that the plane's engine could do the rest, allowing him to fly on to Cheyenne for his come-uppance.

It was noticed that, thereafter, this particular pilot made regular progress reports!

But for the rest of the pilots—the radio-happy ones—they were not only contented, but elated, to continue reporting in over such places as Tie Siding, Jenkin's windmill, Shell Creek—and, of course, Eads Ranch outhouse!

* * *

In current communications even teletype has its lighter moments as may be seen by the following cables that passed between two airline offices in Honolulu and San Francisco: SFO FROM HNL   PAX BAKER FELL ASLEEP DURING FLIGHT WITH SHOES REMOVED STP ON ARRIVAL HNL IN ERROR PUT ON SHOE OF PAX IN NEXT SEAT STP DUE PERFECT FIT PAX DID NOT REALIZE ERROR UNTIL CHECKED IN AT HOTEL STP PLSE CONTACT PAX WHO WAS TRAVELLING ON 26E AND INQUIRE IF HE HOLDING BAKERS SHOE STP BAKER TRAVELLING IN TWO DAYS WILL CLAIM SHOE THEN PLEASE ADV IF PAX IN 26E REQUIRES HIS SHOE BEFORE THEN END.

HNL FROM SFO SEAT 26E WAS UNOCCUPIED ON FLT STP ALL PAX HAD MATCHING SHOES ON ARRIVAL HERE STP ASSUME MR BAKER STARTED TRIP WITH NON MATCHING SHOES OR VISITED PLACE IN HNL AND THERE SHOES SWITCHED STP POSITION NOT NEGATIVE PAX ABLE TO GO BARE FOOT IN HNL END.

* * *

What might be the perfect windup for this chapter involves an incident that took place on a major airline, the planes of which always taxied up to the ramp with a flag flying over the cockpit.

On this occasion, while nearing Pittsburgh, the first officer, for the third or fourth time, asked the captain if he could be of any assistance. The captain, busy with landing procedures and thinking he was using the cockpit interphone, yelled: "Yes, put the flag out, damn it; it looks like we're going to land!"

Right! The captain's priceless statement was heard far and wide over the company air waves!

* * *

Weather, Whether or Not?

Weather conditions often were responsible for the development of hilarious happenings. This was especially so in pre-jet, over-weather flying days. The rigors of winter, for instance, brewed belly laughs at times that would do well in the script of a slapstick comedy.

For instance, in the year 1940 there was no control tower at Kapuskasing, Ontario, and thereby hangs a tale as well as a windsock!

Being mid-winter, the town lay shivering in a minus 15 degree temperature beneath a heavy blanket of snow. On this particular day the weather was anything but a pilot's delight. Visibility was less than a snow-flecked mile and the ceiling was a bare 300 feet.

In the air, Trans-Canada Airlines Flight 2—a Lockheed Lodestar—was approaching "Kap" under the guiding hand of

Trans-Canada Airlines Captain A. R. (Al) Edwards
discovered who the fall guy was at "Kap!"

(TCA Photo)

Old Trans-Canada Airlines (now Air Canada) Lockheed Lodestar (top plane)
and new Air Canada Boeing 727.

Captain Al Edwards.

On the ground TCA's operator, Bill Lucas, doubled, tripled and quadrupled as passenger agent, baggage smasher, radio operator, dispatcher and whatever else it took to run that leg of Trans-Canada.

As lousy as conditions were, Captain Edwards hoped he would not be forced to by-pass "Kap" as it would be a long, miserable haul to the next stop. He'd set her down there with Lucas' help.

"Flight 2 beginning descent at 48," radio'd Al and received Bill's prompt response, "Kap checks Flight 2 beginning descent at 48—going remote."

Now "going remote" meant that Bill bundled into his parka, took a spare headset and microphone and climbed to the roof of Kap's small terminal building. From that perch he would keep Captain Edwards advised of all information pertinent to his approach and landing—ceiling, visibility, wind speed and direction, condition of runway and any other "intelligence" it behooved him to impart.

There was the usual delay while Bill clamored up onto the roof. Finally through Edwards' earphones came the welcome words, "Kap on remote."

Al answered immediately, "O.K.—what's the weather?"

Bill began, "Flight 2 from Kap—the visibility to the north is one-half in snow and the range towers to the west . . . " The voice stopped abruptly. Al frowned. There seemed to be nothing wrong with his radio. What, then, was wrong on Bill's end?

Edwards started a long series of calls, "Flight 2 to Kap! Flight 2 to Kap!" Nothing but vast, or half vast, silence hammered in his ears. "Just wait 'til I get on the ground," breathed Al, as the long minutes passed in continuing silence, "I'll wring his miserable neck!"

Suddenly a breathless voice gasped over the airwaves. "Flight 2 from Kap!"

Captain Edwards, by now as incensed as a bull contronting

his red-caped tormenters,shot back, "Where have you been? And the answer had better be good!"

For a second nothing was audible over the mike but Bill's heavy breathing. Finally, he gasped, "I fell off the roof!"

Sure enough, in moving back for a better look at things, Bill had stepped off the roof and plummeted tail over tea kettle into, fortunately, a large snow bank, therefore precipitating the aggravating delay in communications!

* * *

It was one of those sizzling July evenings before the days of airline radar. Even "upstairs," Captain Howard Reid and First Officer Ken Benson of United Air Lines flying the Denver-Chicago run, could feel the oppressiveness of the atmosphere. They knew only too well that this sort of thing spelled trouble in the form of thunderstorms, always a problem on any flight in those days and this trip promised to be no exception. Already dark cumulus clouds lifted ugly heads far above the flight level. Captain Reid decided to penetrate this area at low altitude and received a clearance at 7,000 feet.

A highly capable, competent pilot, Reid was also a very kindly soul who believed in helping his fellow man, which included his fellow pilot. In this respect he had always made it a practice to let his co-pilot fly half the time in order that he could achieve the necessary experience toward becoming a top-flight captain. So now, since he figured it was Ken's half of the flight, Reid turned the controls over to him and proceeded to sit this one out.

A half-hour after take-off, darkness engulfed them, the blackness of the night being broken only by lightning which highlighted the propellers at each flash. St. Elmo's fire flickered on the glareshield and ahead of the propeller tips like a display of 4th of July fireworks. Ken slowed the DC-6 down to rough air speed and nosed into an area where the lightning appeared less intense but where they were now being pelted by a furious hailstorm. The fearsome staccato of hail lasted briefly, however. Then suddenly a sledgehammer blow struck the aircraft!

Reid cast a quick glance at his partner whose eyes clearly registered the fact that he was not only getting the experience but the "business!" So far, however, he was reacting with captain's precision. Pushing the throttles back and forth, he tried valiantly to keep the airspeed somewhere near 170 m.p.h. and the altitude near 7,000 feet.

Reid, a veteran of many summers of thunderstorms, didn't relish any of the noisy skirmishes but knew that each would be of short duration, the core probably being only five to ten miles across.

The sharp jerks intermittently pushed Ken and Howard deep into their seats and slammed them against their seat belts. With each hard jolt the fuel pressure lights would flicker on and off—seemingly winking at the whole atmospheric turbulence, but this added winking business must have proved a bit too much for Ken.

"What do you think I should do next?" he asked Reid.

Reid tightened his belt still more and hanging on to the glareshield, shouted, "Well, whatever the hell you do, *don't turn back!*"

* * *

Back in the early DC-3 days when the total complement of an airliner consisted of captain, a first officer or co-pilot, one stewardess and up to 21 passengers, rough air (now termed "turbulence") not only played pranks with stomachs but frequently was culpritish in other ways as well. Take it from United Air Lines Captain R. John Wisda, rough air was at least once responsible for a change of directives in UAL's book of rules and regulations.

Wisda recalls this came about on a very hot and sultry day when a stewardess was called on very short notice for duty on a flight to New York. Either because of the heat or, perhaps, lack of time, this air lass neglected to don her panties.

Take it from United Air Lines Captain R. John Wisda a panty-less stewardess hanging from a baggage rack would shake up anybody! (L.A. Airport Photography)

During the course of the trip, the plane encountered un-avoidably severe turbulence at low altitude. The pilots, even though strapped in their seats, had a difficult time maintaining their composure and equilibrium. This vexing problem lasted for quite some time. When the aerial turmoil finally subsided and it was safe to unstrap, the captain, fearful for the welfare of his charges, left his seat and investigated the passenger cabin.

To say he got an eyeful was putting it mildly! The cabin was a nightmarish mess! It was obvious the stewardess had been serving meals at the precise time of the massive turbulence as food was in evidence everywhere—that is, everywhere it *shouldn't* have been. There were fish on the ceiling, scalloped

potatoes plastered on the seats and floor, and vanilla ice cream sloshed about the overhead baggage racks. And that wasn't all!

There, dangling from the baggage racks toward the aft of the cabin, was this cute little stewardess—but unfortunately for her, she was *sans* panties, and *sans* composure!

So it was no surprise, at least to those gleeful witnesses of the "stewardess' hanging," that effective as of that date, a new regulation appeared on the books of United Airlines. Hereafter it was mandatory for all stewardesses to wear panties!

* * *

Northern Switzerland was covered by a large area of storm clouds so it was only natural that the weather radar aboard Finnair's aircraft was full of the radar echoes of storm cells through which Captain Iiro Tamminen and his co-pilot, Mikko Vanhala, threaded their way to Zurich.

At last Captain Tamminen pointed to a radar echo on the screen and said: "Well, *that* isn't a thunder cloud anyway—it's Schaffhausen!"

When the aircraft had passed the echo, with lightning ex-

Finnair Captain Iiro Tamminen appraises the current situation on radar. (Finnair Photo)

citedly playing on all sides, Captain Tamminen turned to Co-pilot Vanhala and said: "It looks as though there's a *power station* at Schaffhausen!"

* * *

5

Trickery

In the years of propeller-driven airliners, novice stewardesses the world over could, at one time or another, expect to become the target of "trickery" perpetrated by fiendish cockpit crews. For the most part such deviltry has been relegated to the past with the advent of stewardess schools and today's jet sky-liners. In the days of the prop jobs, however, as the ensuing incidents illustrate, pilots obviously had more time to concoct satanic schemes as well as aircraft and situations better suited to carry them out.

For starters, there happened aboard an American Airlines Dallas-Fort Worth flight a new stewardess who hailed from New York. Captain Forest M. Johnston and his co-pilot, certain her knowledge of cattle country extended only to what she may have read or had seen in the movies, came up with a gem of an idea. This 28-mile hop allowed them enough time to tell

"Get the passengers in a circle, facing out! Thar's Injuns below!" says American Airlines Captain Forest M. (Iron Hat) Johnston.   (American Airlines Photo)

the new girl they had just been advised by radio that several hundred head of Texas longhorn steers were running amok on the "Cow Town" airport and a dozen or more cowboys were desperately attempting to round them up so they could land. "We might have to circle awhile with this action going on below us," was their straight-faced statement.

The stewardess, still believing in cowboys and Indians, and hardly able to contain herself with excitement, had to immediately inform her passengers over the P.A. system of what was transpiring.

The passengers, mostly Texans, immediately catching on

that their obviously eastern stewardess had become the butt of the pilots' joke, managed to maintain straight faces while inwardly chortling up a storm. All the while one sky-borne stewardess continued looking for the ghost riders on the ground!

* * *

Another new stewardess, also from New York and on her initial trip West, played into the hands of Captain Johnston and his co-pilot as they winged their way over west Texas late one winter evening. They told her they would pass over Indian country on this leg of their flight and would inform her of it when they did.

As darkness descended and the ground disappeared in the blackness of the night, gas flares in the oil fields could be seen hither and yon waving in the late evening breeze. These were pointed out to the stewardess as Indian campfires over which the Indians were cooking their evening meals.

Thrilled to the goose-bump stage with the spectacle, the stewardess rushed aft with the wonderful news. Once again, all-knowing Texan passengers, realizing a prank had been played, chuckled their way to El Paso.

* * *

During World War II, the hot meals served aboard the airliners left much to be desired. Some were good; others were quite the opposite and certainly the butt of many jokes.

In this regard, United Air Lines Captain R. John Wisda came up with a classic incident of the day.

During one of his flights his co-pilot, or first officer, took a "burp-cup" with him to the cockpit. From the gleam in his eyes, it was clear he might have some ulterior motive up his uniformed sleeve.

As the airplane cruised along through smooth air, the co-pilot asked the stewardess to bring his lunch. She complied by carrying his tray to the cockpit, then promptly leaving. Wisda recalls clearly that the day's menu happened to be lamb stew. After the stewardess had departed, the co-pilot, who wasn't really hungry, picked up his new, clean burp-cup and proceeded to deposit the stew, plus some shreds of lettuce in the receptacle. He then placed the cup on the floor by his seat.

In a little while, after some slightly rough air, he called the stewardess, saying he didn't feel well and asked that she bring him a burp-cup. Again she complied and hurriedly left the cockpit.

Some time later she returned to the cockpit to explore the situation and found the captain and co-pilot in exceptionally good humor. In fact, the latter looked so well and sassy, she remarked about it. In reply, the co-pilot, in grandiose manner, said he felt much better—so much so in fact that he thought he now could digest his lunch. Had the stewardess taken stock of that devilish gleam in the pilot's eyes, she would have surmised all was not as it should be but unfortunately she failed to note this detail.

As the stewardess watched, the co-pilot reached down, picked up the previously prepared burp-cup, removed the cap and with a spoon proceeded to devour the contents with gusto.

At this point the stewardess turned as white as a sheet, grabbed the other burp-cup and headed for the john!

* * *

What Captain Geoffrey M. White of Air New Zealand now has to relate proves that on their first flights, airline stewardesses, not only in the United States but all over the world, are targets for pranks played on them by other crew members.

This incident happened while Air New Zealand was still in

"The important thing in flying is to be sure to keep the clouds out of the passenger cabin," avers Air New Zealand Captain Geoffrey M. White.   (Clifton Firth, Ltd., Photo)

its infancy and Captain White was a co-pilot on piston-engined DC-6s. Because of the company's limited staff at that time, training schools for new hostesses, as they are called in New Zealand, were not warranted; therefore their practical training had to be acquired the hard way—aboard the planes. This made the girls even more vulnerable to pilot shenanigans.

Captain White recalls one particular trick played on a hostess, whom we shall call Sue, who received her initial tutoring from a crew that included a long-serving senior steward, whom we shall call Bill. As the DC-6s often flew in and out of clouds around the South Pacific at the relatively low altitudes of 12-18,000 feet, Bill carefully instructed Sue that each time the aircraft neared a cloud, she was to put the plug in the sink in the galley. This, he explained with a straight face, would stop the cloud getting into the aircraft.

Sue, an apt student and very enthusiastic about her new career, followed instructions implicitly. Not a cloud ever made its wispy—if not sneaky—way into the cabin and Sue was triumphant and proud over her success in this unusual "race."

One day toward the end of the flight passengers were keeping her unduly busy and she failed to note the airliner had entered a cloud. When realization dawned, she sped to the galley at top speed and found to her utter dismay that this time she had come out the loser! A mass of white vapor was pouring out of the opening in the sink and already spreading its way into the surrounding galley area. The horrified hostess quickly inserted the plug to halt further seepage of the atmospheric intruder.

Although the frightened and apologetic girl was entirely unaware of the properties of dry ice which the crew had planted to further the prank, she nevertheless received a sound reprimand from Bill who proved more than equal to the occasion. Thereafter Sue was particularly careful to out-race the clouds to the sink.

This episode had its sequel several weeks later when Sue and various members of two or three crews were at a typical after-work gathering of the clan in the crew room of their hotel in Sydney. As usual, there was considerable hangar flying and during the course of which one relatively new steward, who had heard of the incident of the hostess and the plug but who was unaware of her identity, proceeded to recount the joke. It soon became apparent that one young lady present was quietly getting increasingly red in the face as the story progressed and she realized that for some time she had been thoroughly "had."

* * *

In the late '30s, when the DC-3 was the transport of the day and the airlines were more or less still struggling through infancy, often only a sense of humor sustained the employees through many long duty hours. A day was complete for the crew, consisting of captain, co-pilot and stewardess, only if one could pull a good practical joke on someone and particularly if that someone was the stewardess.

On this particular day when the captain reported for a flight he noticed the stewardess was brand spanking new—ideal material for the joke forming in his mind. While he introduced himself to the young woman with stars in her eyes, he explained that he would be quite busy as soon as he boarded the aircraft and to make sure the co-pilot was on board as there would not be time enough for the captain to attend to this particular chore; the co-pilot had a reputation for tardiness, so would she please see to it for him? Being extremely new and eager to please her boss the young lady assured him she would do as he asked. Of course, as he knew, the new "stew" became so snowed under with all the unfamiliar duties of greeting passengers, hanging up coats, etc., she quite forgot to look for the errant co-pilot, who incidentally boarded the aircraft via the baggage loading belt in the nose of the airplane without her knowledge.

Once in the air the co-pilot hid in the front baggage pit while the captain summoned the poor girl who suddenly remembered her oversight. Commanding the sternest expression he could muster, the captain reprimanded her for such an oversight and then surmised they would just have to do without the co-pilot that particular trip; no easy accomplishment either, and a situation that would not contribute much to his good humor.

As soon as they landed at the next station the co-pilot immediately slipped through the front baggage door, rushed to the main cabin door and as soon as it was opened, the first thing to meet the stewardess' eyes was a much disheveled, panting co-pilot who greeted her with, "Boy, you people are sure hard to keep up with!"

* * *

Another of the stunts foisted on stewardesses in the old DC-3 days was to instruct them in the fictitious duty of "raising" the unmovable tailwheel after take-off and "lowering" it prior to landing. This operation, according to the phony instructions, was to take place immediately after the electrically lighted "No Smoking" light was turned off after the plane was airborne. At this time the stewardess was to raise the tailwheel by operating a useless switch in the restroom and then lower it by the same procedure when the "No Smoking" sign came back on prior to landing.

On one flight, after performing her "duty" properly several times and receiving praise for her proficiency, the crew purposely forgot to turn on the smoking sign prior to a landing. Suddenly the panic-stricken stewardess burst into the cockpit, screaming, "*Don't land*! Go around again! Go around again! The tailwheel is still *up*!"

* * *

Still another method of frightening the girls was to set the ship on automatic-pilot and then hide in the baggage pit. After hiding securely, the call-button would be pushed. The stewardess would come to the cockpit and find (1) the pilots gone, and (2) a note reading "Goodbye cruel world" pinned to the control wheel, and (3) the side windows open.

Needless to say, this practice soon came to a halt when a panicked stewardess went screaming back through the cabin and several thoroughly frightened passengers reported the stunt.

* * *

Captain Basil L. Rowe of Pan American World Airways related an incident that happened many years ago when he was flying Sikorsky S-42 flying boats from the Dinner Key base at Coconut Grove, Miami.

"We were just starting on a four-day Rio-Buenos Aires trip," stated Rowe, "and had aboard a flight stewardess from one of the other airlines who was enjoying her first foreign

It's a switch when a stewardess gets juiced in flight. It actually happened on one of Pan-Am Captain Basil Rowe's trips.   (Pan-Am Photo)

PAA Sikorsky S-42 Clipper.

flight, especially when she noted my co-pilot was very handsome. As soon as we were airborne, she lost no time heading for the cockpit to engage in a little romanticism with him which made me quite envious.

"At midday she volunteered to assist the purser in serving lunch. She brought our tomato juice cocktail forward but the one which she handed the co-pilot was generously doctored with Tabasco Sauce. I don't know what she was preparing him for; anyway he couldn't drink it so he set it aside for future use.

"In those old flying boats the flow of air was forward since they flew along with a negative angle. If you opened the cockpit window, everything that wasn't fastened down flew out the window and that frequently included my flight maps.

"Now the ladies' room was just behind the cockpit and the drain for the drinking fountain emptied into the chute for the latrine which opened directly through the bottom of the ship. The co-pilot almost got a stiff neck waiting for the "visiting" stewardess to enter the ladies' room but at last his long watch was rewarded.

"He waited a couple of minutes and then went back and emptied the tomato juice into the drain, returned to his seat and yanked the window open. His timing must have been perfect because you can just imagine the scream that came out of that little girls' room when that tomato juice went *up* the chute instead of *down!*"

* * *

If the foregoing stories are any criterion you should by now know that any new employee, just out of training, joining an airlines crew is a target for some good-natured hazing or initiation into the ranks. Such "rites," especially administered to stewardesses on their first flights, are so cleverly perpetuated that the novice is totally unaware he or she is being hoaxed.

Western Airlines Captain Theodore R. Babbini tells about the so-called initiation a few years ago of one new stewardess

A new stewardess should always check into the best hotels and Western Air Captain Ted Babbini and his crew were always ready to oblige. (Western Air Lines Photo)

on a flight which terminated at Seattle, Washington. It so happened this particular "stew" had never been to Seattle before and did not know the location of the stewardesses' hotel. This gave the captain and his crew a fiendish idea as they had been trying to think of some devilment to play on this latest addition to their "family."

Quite often upon arrival at Seattle, the crew members were able to save on taxi fare to the hotel by driving rental cars left at the airport by customers to their downtown hotels. The crew therefore picked up one of these rental cars and, taking the veteran stewardess into the conspiracy, they drove to a run-down residential hotel for retired male pensioners. There they let the fledgling out, assuring her that was where she was to stay. The other stewardess, knowing of the plot, did not get out, claiming she wanted to go downtown and shop.

The new stewardess, her face mirroring her efforts to hide her disappointment, bravely picked up her bag and marched into the mangy-looking place. Halfway through the lobby, her trim uniform looking weirdly out of place amongst the untidy old bachelors, her courage suddenly deserted her and she fled wildly back to the car. Breathlessly she stated she had decided to go shopping with the other stewardess as there were a few things she had forgotten. The resultant gales of laughter gave the joke away and a much-chagrined, much relieved, far wiser stewardess continued her way to an exceedingly plusher hostelry.

* * *

Captain John W. Kessey of Ansett Airlines of Papua, New Guinea, will vouch for the fact that poor novice stewardesses weren't spared practical jokes even over the far-off southern seas.

He tells of one recruit hostess, making her initial trip on one of Ansett's DC-3s, who was asked to assist with the toilet flushing system. It is a well-known fact that the DC-3, with its old pan-type toilet system, was an ideal airliner for this particular prank. She was told the flushing system had broken down and to assist she was to proceed to the cockpit as fast as possible, each time a passenger left the toilet, and pump furiously on a lever. This action, she was informed, would then flush the toilet. So for the entire flight, the hostess ran her legs off and pumped her arms off each time a passenger answered Nature's call.

The reader thus can well imagine the peppery language that assailed the captain's and first officer's ears when she learned she had been pumping the fuel hand pump and taking care of that little chore for the pilots.

* * *

Another Ansett antic, according to Captain Kessey, was to tell the hostess on board their Fokker Friendship that they were unable to get the wheels down, so would she go to the middle of the cabin and jump furiously up and down in the aisle to help lower the undercarriage.

Naturally, the unsuspecting hostess would always oblige and, of course, the gear was immediately lowered.

The hostess was always extremely pleased in having had a part in releasing the "stuck" landing gear. And it wasn't until some time later that she learned the bitter truth.

* * *

There are times, however, when stewardesses exercise their right to turn the tables and mete out "sauce for the gander," so to speak.

Captain Marui Maunula of Finnair was one captain who eventually had the tables turned on him for a joke he had played on his passengers on a return flight from Palma de Mallorca to Helsinki one April 1st.

He had announced to the passengers over the speaker system that the aircraft was just flying over Copenhagen and that the weather in Helsinki was spring-like with a temperature of 22°C. The passengers reacted with cries of delight and clapping of hands, only to hear the captain say a few seconds later: "April Fool! There's sleet and a temperature of 1°C. in Helsinki."

So it was on a subsequent April Fool's Day Captain Maunula was to suffer a justifiable prank. A stewardess advised him that the president of the company was aboard and that he would like to have a word with the captain.

Captain Maunula hastily straightened his tie, put on his jacket, adjusted his cap and entered the cabin. He slowly walked all the way to the rear of the cabin, studying each face, but saw no president. He returned along the aisle at an even slower pace, scanning each row of passengers minutely. By this time the passengers, who were "in" on the joke, were having a difficult time keeping straight faces. Upon the completion of the puzzled captain's second dry run, the stewardess announced over the loud speaker, "April Fool!"

* * *

Trickery was not always confined to stewardesses, however. Other air crew—and even ground crew— members periodically found themselves victims of deserved, or undeserved, practical jokes.

Boys will be boys even though they have grown up to become airline captains—the very same captains at whom passengers gaze with awe, respect and admiration as they nonchalantly make their way to their respective ships.

As fair proof of this, there is the story of Willy, a United Air Lines captain. Now Willy was an expert in his field and the very epitome of charm and being the exemplary pilot, he believed in adhering strictly to company policies but there were occasions when certain procedures tended to bug him. One in particular was the policy in effect several years ago which, if performed correctly, was calculated to speed up operations in a systematic fashion.

This procedure applied to ramp operations and loading methods. To load an airplane it is necessary to have one man with the authority over all to make certain that all cargo pits and all cargo compartment doors are closed and secured before the plane is cleared to depart the loading area for takeoff.

To expedite matters at that time, the supervisor of this operation was given a whistle with authorization to blow it each time he saw that an airplane was properly loaded. All loading personnel would then evacuate the cargo compartments, slam shut and lock all doors leading to said compartments.

Now, as aforementioned, this whistle rule had a tendency to ruffle Willy's feathers a bit and he figured he would just have to do something about it. A few days later, while sitting in his ship at San Francisco intently watching the ground personnel scurrying about the aircraft, he thought of the impending whistle which would eventually rend the atmosphere like the sound of doom. With rebellion seething deep within him, a diabolical smile began forming on his lips. He was now ready for action—little boy action—but managed to restrain himself until the most opportune time which was during the high point of concentrated activity. Then Willy, his satanic smile broadening perceptibly, calmly reached into his pocket and brought forth a whistle. Putting it to his puckered lips he let loose a blast that must have been heard clear across the airport.

Out of the baggage pits men jumped like rats from a sinking ship! Fuelers hurriedly unhooked their hoses and dashed off in their trucks; half-loaded mail trucks began to roar away, and cargo compartment doors were slammed shut almost in unison. Confusion reigned while the supervisor, his own whistle still in his pocket, apoplectied!

The next day the company confiscated all whistles—even Willy's. The trick had worked, much to Willy's and, probably, most everyone else's complete relief.

* * *

Airline crews, like employees of any other profession, can become rather annoyed by some trait in a fellow worker, particularly if such aggravation is directed at them.

Western Airlines Captain Theodore R. Babbini recalls a trait of a fellow captain which was a constant source of irritation to the rest of the crew, especially the flight engineers. Because the captain was inclined to be somewhat of a martinet; he did everything "by the book." For instance, on long monotonous night flights, he would suddenly whip his head around to see if he could catch the flight engineers snatching a clandestine 40 winks. Of course this kept the engineers on their proverbial toes but the implied lack of trust soon got under their respective hides. At long last, having decided they'd had it with this captain, one of the more intrepid of the flight engineers decided to bring it to a grinding halt.

To cure the captain of his irritating habit, the engineer quietly prepared a trap for him. One night, as the plane droned along and the cockpit was quiet, the captain, as usual, decided to pull his little nap check—and nearly jumped out of his seat!

KLM Captain W. Van Veenendaal finds himself all tied up with an Indonesian operating on a shoestring. (KLM Photo)

He found himself staring into the leering grimace of a horrible rubber Hallowe'en mask!

It was now the captain's turn to become riled. Upon landing he immediately filed a complaint against the "brazen" flight engineer but received little satisfaction for his efforts—the punishment meted being just a mild tap on the wrist for the engineer and gales of laughter for the captain!

* * *

Not all captains' woes occur in flight. Quite often they occur on the ground, and even then they are sometimes too tied up to do anything about it. One who will vociferously vouch for that is Captain W. Van Veenendaal of KLM Royal Dutch Airlines.

His illustrative incident occurred upon the successful completion of one of the good captain's Amsterdam-Djakarta flights, when he decided a shoeshine might give his already high morale a still further lift before venturing into one of the better cafes of that Indonesian capital. He therefore accepted the services of one of the interminable number of little shoeshine boys along the streets, picking one particular eager beaver whose outstretched hands, bright eyes and matching smile had quickly won him over.

Now these young "business men," though uneducated, become surprisingly keen in the ways of business. One phase of this so-called business acumen, however, can be very annoying to the customers. Many of these native small fry quickly learn that a certain amount of astuteness—although thievery might be the better word—frequently can produce a bit of extra revenue. Apparently our flying Dutchman was totally unaware of the connivance of these innocent-appearing imps.

As the youngster he hired was slapping his brogues to a super-shiny finish, Van Veenendaal made the discovery that he had no change, only a pound note. The boy obligingly offered to change the pound, stating it wouldn't take long as he could get it "right over there" and assuringly adding that he'd be "right back."

Van Veenendaal noted that the youngster not only went "right over there," but kept right on going. For a minute Van Veenendaal didn't comprehend the significance of this lightning move. When he finally realized he'd been taken, he became furious. He decided to teach the little brat a lesson. In his attempt to make a wild dash after the absconder, something happened which he had not anticipated but which the wily shoeshiner had. At his first step, Van Veenendaal made a beaut of a one-point crash-landing—right on his nose!

The boy had evolved a diabolically clever way of securing that little extra revenue. He had tied Van Veenendaal's shoelaces together!

* * *

One captain of British Overseas Airways used to regard himself with pride as an English teacher of considerable ability and nothing gave him more pleasure than trying out his prowess on the little boys and girls operating elevators, or lifts, in Tokyo hotels. Were it not known before, by then one would have discovered the captain also had a keen sense of humor as his English lessons sometimes took an odd quirk. For instance, the captain taught these youths the names of some of London's fashionable stores pretending that names like "Harrods" and "Bourne and Hollingsworth" were polite greetings. As the Japanese are a courteous race, the children eagerly learned all of the captain's various phony greetings and immediately employed them in their work.

The results of these unique salutations were some very perplexed Japanese guests. One of the captain's BOAC colleagues who used to fly the routes with him recalls going up and down in lifts in several Tokyo hotels shortly thereafter with puzzled guests listening to the young elevator operators chanting "Debenham and Freebodys!" at every floor.

It was months later when the captain's colleague again checked into a hotel at Tokyo after a flight from Hong Kong. After signing the register he thought he would have a shower before finding out which BOAC crews were also staying in Tokyo. By now he had forgotten all about a certain captain's English tutoring.

The incident of the lessons, however, was quickly brought back to mind when he stepped into the hotel lift only to be greeted by the elevator boy's cry: "Fortnum and Mason!" It was quite unnecessary now to check on the BOAC flight crew—he immediately *knew* who was in town!

* * *

Pilot C. E. Ambrose of Canadian Pacific Air recounts an episode which created quite a tizzy in a fasionable hostelry in Singapore, in which city he resided at the time.

In 1966 British Eagle crews stayed at Singapore's very

According to Canadian Pacific Airlines Captain C. E. Ambrose, it isn't often one meets a "corpse" in an elevator—even in Singapore.
(Canadian Pacific Airlines Photo)

smart hotel, Singapura International—the "in" place to stay. One evening an entire crew, including a friend of Pilot Ambrose's, eager to relax and have fun, went out to take in Bugis Street as well as other fleshpot areas of the city.

After the festivities, they returned to the hotel in a more or less well-oiled condition; in fact, the flight engineer was lubricated to the point that he had to be assisted to his room. En route someone mischievously collected a linen trolley. In his room, the engineer, now quite unconcious, was undressed, laid on the cart and very thoughtfully covered with a sheet. Then, as though administering the coupe de grace, the engineer's pals wheeled the trolley with its reclining "cadaver" into the elevator and pushed the ground floor button.

In the lobby a gaggle of elderly American tourists had just returned from their evening on the town. Unfortunately for all concerned, especially for the engineer, the Americans arrived in far better condition than the fly boys. They therefore were totally unprepared for the inevitable. They met the engineer!

The aftermath of this night's fun and frolic was immediate banishment of the British Eagle crew to a hotel miles away in Katong!

* * *

But for one or two instances, stewardesses have been given a poor shake in the preceding pages; however they weren't all that gullible. Often, once stung, they became the stingers.

A perfect example of this happened aboard a United Air Lines tri-motored Boeing 80-A a number of years ago. The captain, who shall remain anonymous, had a habit of slapping and grabbing the stewardesses' legs when they would sit on the mid jump seat in the 80-As.

Finally one stewardess, having had enough of this tom-foolery, put a stop to the business in a most novel manner. She put a garter above her knee with several thumb tacks in it—pointing out!

* * *

Even passengers themselves get into the act.

According to one Western Air Lines captain, who related this story with no little glee, a seasoned airline traveler of his acquaintance who doesn't mind being named—Neal Cole of Oak Grove, Oregon—who seemingly possesses an un-checkable penchant for wild stories, was on something like his 22nd flight to Honolulu on one airline or another. However, this time Cole was aboard Western and seated next to two of what he dubbed "old maid school teacher types" who, quite apparently, were on their very first airline trip.

About half way to Honolulu, Cole struck up a conversation with the ladies by casually mentioning that Western Air Lines was a very fine airline in many respects but that the only thing he disliked about the line was that they lost too many women and children on their transocean flights.

Quite naturally taken aback, the ladies inquired as to how on earth he could have come to that conclusion.

"Because", answered Cole, "when trouble arises they always toss them out first. Then, somehow, the trouble corrects itself and the plane makes it on to Honolulu with only the men passengers aboard!"

After thinking this over and quietly discussing it for a few moments, one of the ladies worriedly inquired:

"Do you think our pilot might relax those rules on this trip?"

* * *

On another Western Air Lines flight to Honolulu aboard a 747, Cole happened to be in the lounge sipping a martini or two. Each time he was served a drink he would jot down a note in a small note book. A fellow passenger, eyeing this strange procedure, asked Cole why he entered a note each time a drink was served.

"Well", answered Cole with the usual tongue-in-cheek, "I'm keeping track of every shot of Vodka and every olive I consume on these trips for income tax purposes. Do you know that, in 22 years of these flights to Hawaii, I've gone thru over 13 gallons of Vodka and a 55-gallon drum of olives?"

With a strange wild look the passenger backed off and headed for his seat. Shortly a stewardess approached Cole with a wide grin and asked how on earth—or in the air—did he ever manage to concoct such wild stories with which to confound his fellow passengers? This one, said she, had gone the entire rounds of the plane.

"But", quoth the stewardess, "It's things like this that make my day!"

* * *

The Singing Captain

As all airline passengers know, it is customery for the captain to usually greet them over the public address system with, "This is your captain speaking," then enter on a discourse as to altitude at which they will fly; speed of the aircraft; places of interest they will see; weather conditions they can expect to encounter, and whatever other information upon which he sees fit to expound.

One captain on El Al, Israel's national airline, however, employs an entirely different modus operandi. He's Captain Leo Gardner whose deviation from the usual is quite surprising—even startling. But then Captain Gardner is not the usual type of captain. A man of many talents, his unusual background in itself would make a book well worth the reading.

First of all, Gardner is blessed with an outstanding singing

EL AL ISRAEL AIRLINES

voice. The son of a New Hampshire rabbi and cantor, he began singing in his synagogue choir at the ripe old age of five. By the time he was nine he was helping to conduct services and, together with his two brothers and father, did service as tenor in the synagogue quartette.

At 10 years of age he began driving a car; at 12, by twisting the truth a bit, he received his license; at 14 he had learned to fly. Also during this teenage period he accummulated quite a reputation as a motorcyclist, along with his friend, Sam Lewis, one of the founders of El Al who subsequently became its chief pilot.

When Gardner was 18, he and his two brothers sang as a trio on CBS' nine-state radio network from San Francisco and did a series of 50 recordings for transcription and radio commercials.

He could not, however, see himself in a starring artist's role, so at the advent of World War II he returned to what by then was his first love—flying—and became a flight instructor in Arizona. One of his students was the famous actor, John Payne, whose shoulders were so broad that when he got into the cockpit, Gardner complained Payne completely blocked his view. Quite possibly that was one reason why Gardner later

122

EL AL Captain Sam Lewis, left, and EL AL's "Singing Captain", Leo Gardner, right, center captain unidentified.

entered the Air Transport Command and flew bombers to all theatres. At least his view wasn't blocked!

In 1950 Gardner began flying for El Al Airlines, joining his boyhood friend, Sam Lewis, a gifted pianist. And thus something unique was born for El Al, since, in addition to his other accomplishments, Captain Gardner is also an expert linguist, fluently speaking French, Italian, German, Yiddish, Hebrew and English, he decided to combine these talents with his daily duties as an airline captain.

Captain Gardner vividly remembers that first flight when he put his idea into effect. He was at the controls of a DC-4 out of Tel Aviv en route to Rome and London. It was an extremely

hot day and there was no airconditioning in the DC-4. The atmosphere became almost unbearably sticky. The passengers, mopping their damp faces, began to resemble a stand of wilted vegetables. With the DC-4 trimmed away and droning smoothly at 9,500 feet, Captain Gardner suddenly thought of a remedial measure which he hoped would to some extent allay the discomforture of the passengers by diverting their minds to other things.

Picking up the mike, he made this surprising announcement over the P.A. system: "This is your captain speaking. You might enjoy a little vocalization to get your mind on nicer things than the heat—this is just a little extra service that El Al, and *only* El Al, gives!"

With that he burst into song! He was such an instantaneous hit, the cabin attendants were kept on the hop bringing him requests from the passengers. Having a tremendous repertoire, Gardner had no difficulty obliging, singing ballads, classics or operatic arias with equal professional ease.

From then on the *singing captain* was a regular feature of El Al flights—and sometimes it even turned out to be a double feature! That's when Gardner and Lewis flew together. Lewis, an artist on the ivories, always had a mobile piano put aboard so they could perform as a musical duo, and they made quite a team. Groups from various countries were delighted to have Gardner serenade them in their own language. Usually when flying over Rome, he would render an Italian aria; he was even undaunted singing his way over Africa though he knew not a note of Swahili! As for Lewis, he could tickle the ivories in any language. Unfortunately, however, these boyhood friends rarely got to fly with each other.

Because of these musical captains, El Al has the distinction of being the first airline anywhere to offer in-flight entertainment to its passengers.

So if any of you ever board an El Al airliner, don't be surprised if, over the P.A. system, you should hear this greeting, "This is your captain singing!"

* * *

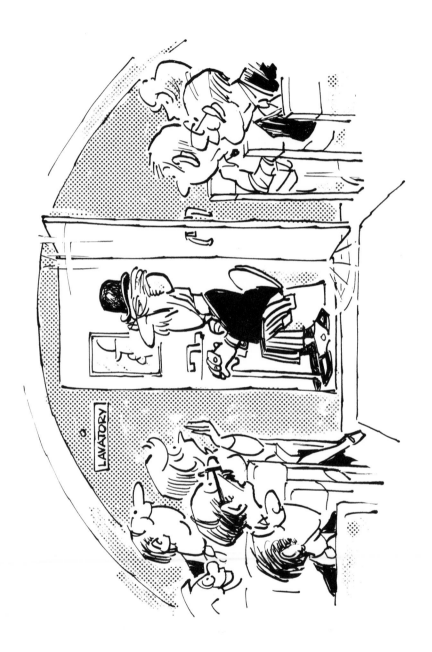

Blue Room

Ever since lavatories were installed on airliners, these relief rooms have been generally known in the industry as "Blue Rooms." Now there probably is a good reason for this, one which we have somehow failed to delve into. However, from the following incidents it is our candid opinion that airline restrooms should be designated as "Red Rooms" rather than "Blue Rooms" since red signifies danger, and using these facilities, as you shall see, can be somewhat of a risky business indeed.

When an airline pilot leaves his official perch to check how things are going back in the cabin, it is not always an uninteresting trek. He sometimes witnesses astounding incidents that could have come right out of a Laurel and Hardy comedy.

American Airlines Captain Forest M. Johnston came upon a real eyebrow-raiser when nearing the end of a Tulsa-New

York flight he decided to check on the passengers and also have a cup of coffee while at the rear of the aircraft.

"I had just asked for cream in my coffee," said he, "and was talking to a school teacher who was making her first flight, when all of a sudden the aircraft took a big bounce and the toilet door banged wide open! In an instant all passengers were alert and looking in the direction of the captain and stewardess—and at the same time and more importantly at a gentleman seated in the toilet staring at an airplane load of passengers!

"All was quiet for several seconds while the man stared at the passengers and vice versa, then suddenly the man in the embarrassing situation, and obviously English from dress and partial undress and speech, straightened into an upright position in an effort to assume a very dignified mien. Then, very nonchalantly, he extended his arm towards the passengers and made a half circle movement, palm toward his audience, and called, "Hi, ya people!" At the same instant he grabbed the door and slammed it shut.

"There was a great collective guffaw from everyone but the school teacher whose face had turned fireball red as she was closest to the toilet and almost looking eyeball to eyeball at the No. 1 actor. Turning to me she said, 'Thank goodness, I can still blush!' No one knew if the gentleman in the "Blue Room" blushed but it is anyone's guess he did."

* * *

Here is another almost unbelievable situation but Captain Frank L. Swaim can attest to its credibility.

It occurred on one of United Air Lines' DC-3s which Swaim was captaining. An elderly man had gone to the "Blue Room" in the rear of the cabin. Shortly thereafter an elderly lady asked the stewardess to assist her back to the said room and the stewardess obligingly did.

Upon opening the unlocked door they confronted the little old man. The stewardess became more than a little flustered and in her utter embarrassment, she "formally" introduced

The Douglas DC-3 used by United Airlines for many pre-World War II years.

the man and woman. The confusion of the poor fellow attempting to be polite and stand up in a lady's presence with his pants at half mast was rather riotous to say the least.

* * *

Much credit must be accorded stewardesses—those glamour gals of the skyways—who are indeed an integral part of airline travel, performing services in countless ways to make passengers comfortable and happy. In one instance, however, one of these sky-belles was given credit for a nicety she had not rendered and until the male passenger involved should happen to see this, he undoubtedly will continue to give that stewardess all due credit for "services rendered."

This episode happened when Basil L. Rowe of Pan American World Airways was captain of a Douglas DC-6 flight crew from the Canal Zone to Miami which consisted of co-pilot, flight engineer, two beautiful stewardesses and himself. His report states:

"Taking off from the south runway we climbed rapidly to our cruising altitude of 15,000 feet which was high above the scattered cumulus and rough air of the cloud level. After leveling off, I turned on the automatic pilot and rolled my seat back to a comfortable position to stretch my legs. Some time later one of the stewardesses entered the cockpit so imbibed with humor that she could hardly talk. And here is the sequence of events that provided the humor.

"A woman with her son occupied two side-by-side seats at the midway point of the cabin. Ahead of her sat a man and his wife. The woman and son went forward to the restrooms located amidships, she taking the port restroom while the son entered the room across the aisle. The son occupied the room for only a few minutes and came back to his seat. The man occupying the next seat ahead got up and went to the restroom which the boy had just vacated. A few minutes later the woman came out of the restroom, and thinking her son was still there, cracked the door and said something, after which she returned to her seat. Observing her son in his seat, her mouth flew open and she plopped into her seat, grabbing up a magazine behind which to hide her face.

"When the man returned to his seat, he said to his wife, 'These stewardesses always surprise me. Do you know what that girl said when she cracked open the door? She said, 'DON'T FORGET YOUR ZIPPER!' "

* * *

Like the man on the Boston subway "who never returned," uncountable numbers of airline passengers for various reasons enter the "Blue Rooms" of airliners and seemingly never return—at least until rescue operations are instigated by the crew.

Consider, thus, the well turned-out man in his early 60s traveling with his son on a Trans-Canada Airlines flight piloted by Captain R. J. Baker, engineering test pilot of TCL.

Somewhere out of Montreal, en route to London, the aforementioned gentlemen found such a trek imperative. After 20 minutes or so, the purser noted that the man's sojourn was developing into an unduly long time and thought he had better consult with the son. The latter felt certain nothing was amiss;

130

that his father often spent longer-than-ordinary periods of time in restrooms and that he would emerge shortly. Tempus fidgeted, as did the purser and several passengers who also felt "Blue Room" calls developing, so after another consultation with the son, it was decided a check should be made.

Receiving no response to their knocks upon the locked door, the door was forced open, and the predicament in which they found the "inmate" shouldn't have happened to Satan himself!

The occupant was on his knees, unable to rise, with his head half-way into the bowl. His face bore a feverish look, but airsickness had nothing to do with either his position or flushed countenance.

Apparently he had decided to light a cigarette while standing before the bowl and his highly-prized lighter had slipped from his hand and dropped into the receptacle. In diving after it, he'd gotten his hand through the lower opening just as the then-new automatic trap was closing.

It had caught his wrist and no amount of pulling could unjohn the gent. In this awkward position, he was unable to get his other hand inside the bowl. Snared like a trapped hare, there was nothing he could do but await rescue which, he knew, would prove a major project at best. Without a doubt this was his most embarrassing moment and he fervently hoped his fellow passengers would not get wind of his plight.

The purser and son worked feverishly in an attempt to release the man's arm from the vice-like grip but got nowhere fast. That this operation would prove a major project was the understatement of the year. There was but one thing to do—SOS for additional help.

Soon the little room was fairly bulging with uniformed personnel, and those who couldn't squeeze in kibitzed from the aisle. At long last extrication was achieved and the hapless, chagrined passenger returned to his seat.

It seemed, however, that having to be rescued from such an unorthodox predicament was not his only embarrassment. To make matters worse, when he'd gone to the men's "Blue Room" and found it in use, he'd slipped into the one marked "Ladies!"

"Imagine," groaned he, ruefully nursing his sore wrist, "trapped in a ladies' restroom! I'll never live *THAT* down!"

* * *

When the DC-6, one of the first airliners that could be pressurized, came into use, the difference in pressures caused no end of trouble with the lavatory flushing system, and one thing the engineers hadn't counted on was the heavyweight air traveler.

On one occasion a decidedly overweight woman went into the restroom and, as is the natural custom for women, sat down on the seat. Due to her obesity, the fat around her posterior created a strong suction seal. The result was that she found it impossible to arise from her seated position without assistance which, in her embarrassing predicament, was no easy thing to call for. After a half hour or so of attempting to accumulate enough nerve to call out, a stewardess who had noticed her enter the restroom and who had become concerned when she failed to come out after so long a time, knocked on the door and asked if she were okay.

"Get me out of here! I'm stuck on the pot!" she fairly screamed!

The stewardess tugged until she was blue in the face—all to no avail. She then enlisted the aid of the second stewardess with the same negative result. At this point the co-pilot was called into the act, and the impasse—as well as the suction—was broken with all four of them catapulting out of the restroom into the cabin aisle in a most undignified heap! Quite a sight to say the least!

* * *

A like instance of stick-to-itiveness by an airline passenger in the "Blue Room" happened aboard a Western airliner.

Captain Theodore R. Babbini of Western relates this tale of

Douglas DC-6B, (1952).

"Blue Room" woe which happened as his DC-6 was tooling along at 18,000 feet.

Unknown to the crew, the toilet in the lavatory had developed an air leak. An elderly lady, feeling the call of Nature, went back and settled herself upon the seat. When she attempted to rise, she found herself gripped fast by the suction.

After struggling for a few minutes in vain, she finally called the stewardess. The stewardess was just as unsuccessful in pulling the passenger off the seat so they finally enlisted the aid of the flight engineer.

It took the combined efforts of both the stewardess and the engineer to haul the poor old lady off the pot!

* * *

Crazy happenings aboard airliners were not always initiated by man. Sometimes the aircraft itself was a major factor in producing hilarious situations.

Although this did not happen on his flight, Zay Smith, who

United Airlines tri-motored Boeing 80-A Passenger planes used during the 1930's. City is Chicago.

started flying with United Air Lines as first officer in 1933, clearly remembers one such incident that occurred the summer of that year and which was the story of the month. At that time there were still some of the tri-motored Boeing 80-A planes around with a canvas wall separating the luggage space from the washroom compartment. This setup afforded at least one passenger the scare of his life.

It happened on a Chicago to New York flight when a male passenger went to the "Blue Room."

"Screams from the 'john'." relates Smith, "brought the stewardess on the run. 'Help, help! I'm falling out of the plane!' The stewardess rushed to the cockpit and asked the co-pilot to bring the key to the toilet compartment. When he opened the door, the co-pilot saw a man with his feet on the 'john' and his fanny sticking through the zippered canvas wall separating the washroom from the baggage compartment. In a cold sweat of fear he was hanging on for dear life with his out-stretched arms against the canvas wall. The cold air on his exposed rear end convinced him that when the plane had hit a

134

rough bump, he had been thrown against the outer wall of the plane and that he was about to fall through the ruptured wall to the ground thousands of feet below. The co-pilot pulled him into the room and pointed to a suitcase only an inch or so below where he had been."

* * *

Another situation, more serious than humorous, that kept the "Blue Rooms" working at peak capacity happened one day on a Northwest Airlines flight from Billings to Minneapolis.

Captain Joe Kimm and First Officer Tommy Chastain had just reached a cruising altitude of 11,000 feet when they realized all was not as it should be. It was discovered the landing gear had dropped half way down, indicating a hydraulic failure of the *up* lines. Captain Kimm immediately swung his Northwest Airlines Lockheed around and headed back to Billings, all the while trying to lower the gear with the emergency system but it was like trying to force a balky jackass off his hind end after his front end had been made up! Since a mechanic was not aboard, it was up to them to do something about this unholy situation. The only tools on the plane were a file, a hammer and a pair of pliers which were not exactly a pilot's "bill of fare." And repairing a faulty hydraulic system certainly wasn't in his line, either. Kimm and Chastain realized they needed assistance but it was obvious whatever help they could get would have to be via radio. They therefore aired their predicament to both NWA's Billings and Minneapolis bases.

The maintenance crew at the Minneapolis shop immediately furnished instructions as to the best possible use of the three tools available. First they were to sever the large hydraulic line with the file, then bend and crimp it with the hammer and pliers. This separated the power system from the hand-pump system and also isolated the *up* system from the *down* system, allowing the build-up of pressure on the *down* side. Now this

135

sounded simple enough but with only the three stated tools with which to work, this mechanical business took a full four and a half hours of hard work, plus a lot of sweat and some salty language, while endlessly circling the Billings Airport.

During this feat of ingenuity they lost all of their hydraulic fluid; therefore upon completion of the temporary modification to the system, they were faced with the added problem of replenishing the supply of fluid. By rummaging through the kitchenette, Chastain hauled out all of the ship's water, coffee and even a thermos of hot chocolate which they had purchased in the Billings Airport cafe. With these liquids they managed to get one of the gears down and locked. Now there was still the other gear to lower but they had run out of fluid, and the next procedure was to confiscate any and all liquid in reachable luggage, but a drier load of passengers there never was! Since they were rapidly running out of fuel, there was but one solution to avoid a crash-landing—personal "contributions"—and we mean "personal" with a capital "P!" Without a doubt, the situation had taken a most delicate turn, as well as a dangerous one, but the latter by far took precedence over the former.

After each of the crew had "contributed" what fluid they could muster after a trip to the little boy's room, they were faced with the not so easy task of making a like request of the passengers, but who was to do the asking? Kimm said Chastain should do it. Chastain said Kimm should do it. After all, *he* was captain of the ship! Finally, they decided to compromise as there was no time to argue the point, so Kimm took the plunge. Would the passengers please "contribute" to save their necks? They would—and did—while Chastain did the "collecting." With the added fluid the crew was able to pump down and lock the other gear, after which they landed safely with just 15 minutes of fuel remaining. If any of the passengers claimed they helped land that aircraft, they certainly weren't *kid*neying!

* * *

No Cure For
a (Wrong) Code

During World War II code books were used by airlines in order to approach, pass or land at various U.S. military installations.

For security reasons a brand new code book was issued each day. These generally consisted of a loose-leaf note book of approximately 100 pages in which, among other things, instructions were given on which way to turn, depending on the GCT (Greenwich Civil Time); at which altitude, and over which particular point. For instance, without this daily code no aircraft could approach Honolulu's Hickam Field without a brace of Marine gunners taking a well-aimed double-A pot shot at the offending craft.

Bear this in mind as this particular day in the life of former United Air Lines Captain G. C. Kehmeier, then a first officer, began.

Former United Air Lines Captain G. C. Kehmeier learned early that you should smell it, too—it could be soy sauce.

The moon shone brightly over Canton Island. First Officer Kehmeier could hear the clump-clump of heavy boots crunching the coral. A few moments later the screen door popped open and a light snapped on.

"Rise and shine! You're due off in an hour," called out the Officer of the Day cheerfully, almost gleefully, as he slammed the screen.

There ought to be a law, thought Kehmeier darkly, squinting up at the O.D. Rise and shine, indeed! He'd manage to rise all right but the extent of his "shine" at this ungodly hour could only be compared to the efforts of the 25-watt bulb glowing spiritlessly from the ceiling.

Thirty minutes later, Kehmeier, his eyes still at half mast, picked up the code for the day at the radio shack. After signing for it, Kehmeier stumbled to the mess hall to enjoy—or he was supposed to—some gluey oatmeal and Spam. "And 20 years later," he vows, "I still hate the stuff!" The coffee, though, was good and probably accounted for the world looking at least slightly brighter as he ascended the steps to the C-87.

Leaving Canton's long runway, the plane grumbled over the dark sea as Captain George Douglass "tied" the controls together for a slow, climbing turn toward Honolulu 1,800 miles northward.

Shortly after 1500 hours GCT dawn began to break. Simultaneously Kehmeier began going over the various codes, procedures and approach plates to be used when they landed about noon. It was soon apparent there was something rotten much closer than Denmark. "I think," said he to the captain, "I've got the wrong code." As Captain Douglass reached for it, he hoped Kehmeier didn't know what he was talking about but a hasty check verified the fact that it certainly was the wrong code. It was for the preceding day! The radio operator must have been as sleepy as Kehmeier to have goofed so outlandishly.

The captain turned to Jim Donovan, the radio operator. "When we are 15 minutes out, call Hickam Tower and tell them we need a straight-in approach." He figured there was no point in trying to out-guess the code and invite disaster from some itchy-fingered Marine gunner at Barbers Point.

The tower gave straight-in clearance without question so upon their arrival at Honolulu they were hardly prepared for the reception committee that met them at the end of the landing roll. Said committee consisted of several armed trucks with machine guns mounted—and what was worse, aimed their way by several eager-beaverish looking younsters. A colonel, also eager and important-looking, escorted them via a staff car into an interrogation room. The door closed and the colonel took over, supported by two aides, a major and a lieutenant. The colonel eyed them haughtily. Judging from his attitude, he must have been an academy man who was awed by the great responsibility of his present command—that of flying a mahogany desk.

"Why," the august one began, "did you ask for a straight-in

approach?"

Since Kehmeier felt he was responsible for the whole mess, he replied, "I got the wrong code from the radio operator at Canton. In the circumstances it appeared the most reasonable thing to do."

Captain Douglass interrupted with, "Colonel, I was in command of this flight. Anything that was done by one of my crew was *my* mistake. Please address your remarks to me."

The colonel seemed taken aback by this direct order. "Very well," he snorted. "Prior to take-off, you must check a few items, such as radio code for the day, don't you?"

"I expect the Air Corps to give me the proper code," the captain replied evenly.

The colonel bristled. "But codes are *important*, captain! Surely you check your *fuel* before take-off?"

Captain Douglass looked levelly at the superior desk pilot who waited with an expression that clearly said the answer had better be good! There was a static silence, then with slow verbal strides, Douglass replied, "Colonel, I *check* the gauges to see that the tanks show full. I don't *taste* the fuel! It could be *water!*"

The meeting adjourned.

* * *

9

T. W. What??

The airline serving the Orkney Islands is Loganair, probably the world's only airline whose planes, more often than not, land backwards. This is because Orkney has the dubious distinction of being the windiest place in Britain. Most winters will have blows topping 90 m.p.h. and in 1969 the wind set a howling record of 136 m.p.h. Accordingly, high winds and rough fields are accepted hazards by Loganair which for years has been serving—backwards or forwards—the remote and rugged Orkney North Isles. Until 500 years ago, when they became a part of Britain, the Orkneys were a part of Scandinavia, upon whom they are still blaming the wind.

Although Loganair—which, believe it or not, is sometimes known as "T.W.A. Orkney," the letters standing for "Teeny Weeny Airlines"—is a very small self-contained airline system with but one plane at this writing—a Britten Norman

141

Britten-Norman "Islander" of Loganair.

"Islander"—and two pilots, the scope of its operations is tremendous.

Loganair operates regularly scheduled services linking seven of the Orkneys—Eday, Westray, Papa Westray, Stronsay, Sanday and North Ronaldsay—with Kirkwall on the main island of Orkney. The population of these islands, between 140 and 900 people each, has come to regard Loganair's operations as an integral and valued part of their daily life.

Now, normally, during strong winds, Loganair pilots increase their indicated airspeed when landing so as to give themselves reasonable forward ground speed—say about 20 m.p.h. The islanders, however, have become used to the buffeting of the aircraft which they have found is better than lurching about on a boat for hours on end.

On occasion Loganair's pilots actually will come in to land backwards—just for amusement. This is quite possible if, for instance, there is an easterly 70 m.p.h. wind and the Islander is flying quite happily at 60 m.p.h. I.A.S.

To bring the ship in for such a reverse landing, Loganair pilots start at the end of the airstrip where normally the landing would have terminated. Then at the speedy rate of 10 m.p.h., the plane is flown backwards to the opposite end of the

runway where normally it would have started touch-down.

Naturally these uneventful, though most unusual, landings are more than a little confusing to the passengers, especially to one particular awe-stricken fellow, a local crofter.

Upon deplaning, he looked gratefully at his pilot and said, "Ye had trouble getting her doon that time, Cap'n . . . . . Thorrt I was going to emygrate to Ameryca!"

Flying backwards, however, is not Loganair's only claim to fame. Loganair also operates what it claims to be the world's shortest scheduled air service. This is between the island of Westray and Papa Westray which is scheduled as a two-minute flight but which, in fact, can take as little as one minute and ten seconds. The distance involved from one airstrip to another is about two-thirds of the length of the longest runway at Heathrow—London's airport.

Perhaps it can also be said that Loganair operates the world's second shortest scheduled air route—four minutes—between the islands of Stronsay and Sanday. The airline's longest scheduled flight? Thirteen minutes.

What, you may ask, does such a comparatively diminuitive airline do for business on these two-breath routes? Well, one might say that the company's twin-engined "Islander" literally circulates life around the islands, carrying teachers to isolated schools; mechanics to broken-down farm equipment; out-patients to hospitals; press cameramen to news spots; sky

143

"Twenty miles an hour? Oh, that's about 40 miles an hour faster than we usually land!" says Loganair Captain A. D. Alsop.(Loganair Photo)

divers to their parachute clubs, and rendering such other necessary services as the transportation of cargo—anything from live lobsters bound for London to a bicycle bound for, say, Ronaldsay!

Much to the amusement of the localites, a certain flight departure announcement always puzzles tourists and other passengers not in the so-called know. It's the announcement of the departure of flight such and such to various small Orkney Islands and "London Airport." The "London Airport" referred to in the announcement is not situated in England but on the island of Eday where the airstrip happens to be in a village actually called London.

Considering the rugged and isolated terrain, and weather conditions, Loganair's operation is really bush flying. Frequent bad weather forces the pilots to navigate by the headlands, farms and other landmarks they can detect through the murk. Flying from Kirkwall on a cloudy day, for instance, can be really quite dramatic. Telephone calls are made to the helpers on the airstrips to check whether conditions there will allow a landing. It seems that if they can see more than a dozen sheep, it's all clear and off one goes!

In Britain, and probably in Europe, Loganair is the only airline flying regularly scheduled public transport services whose winter uniform for the pilots includes Wellington boots! These are necessitated by the fact that the six outlying airfields, except Kirkwall Airport, are just ordinary farm fields with the stones removed which have runways marked out on them, a bit of extra drainage put in where necessary, a wooden hut to house a fire trailer and any waiting passengers, plus a telephone. Because some of these fields yield a healthy silage crop, the effects of a Scottish winter on grass airstrips really makes the rubber boots a must.

Loganair probably also is the only airline in the world that must share its runway with livestock other than rabbits. That's because when flying operations are not in progress, the "airports," aside from those growing silage crops, revert to time-honored pastoral use—normally grazing cattle or sheep. In fact, many times livestock are still on the airstrips and must be chased off before a landing can be made. All of this, however, is taken in stride by the pilots, along with the fact that their aircraft frequently returns from a flight incognito—and, again, it's probably the only airliner in the world that does! From the following you can readily understand why.

Since the whole of Orkney's economy is based on rearing beef cattle, virtually all the grass is used for this purpose, including that on the airstrips. What happens is that 10 minutes or so before the first landing at a particular island each day, the cattle are cleared off the airstrip and are allowed to return shortly after the last landing of the day. In the spring, when the grass is lush, this presents quite a problem as the cows eat it with relish only to suffer from diarrhea! For Loganair, this means utter disaster for its shiny red and white-trimmed Islander which gets plastered from top to bottom with sharne (local Orkney name for cow dung) splashed up by the wheels and propellers. In the spring and summer when Loganair's schedule calls for some 40 landings per day, the aircraft quickly becomes an unrecognizable mess!

145

Some of Loganair's Orkney based staff with one of their aircraft ("Islander") at Kirkwall Airport in Orkney.

Back when Loganair was initiating its service in Orkney, this odoriferous situation seemed to irk one British aircraft inspector no end. The company was having enough trouble as it was with so much official "red tape" constantly getting in the way although this proposed type of flying had been done in pre-war "barnstorming" days. Since then, however, no one had tried to get this sort of operation past the Board of Trade which then was responsible for British civil aviation. After much argument the Board agreed that the operation was sound in principal but said that it would have to be demonstrated fully to their inspectors.

Eventually the day for the demonstration came and after much pouring over the Loganair's Islander, it set off to prove itself around the isles. Various things were not quite right:

Inspector: "Shouldn't you add a 10% increment (amount of increase) for landing on wet grass?" - 01°:
"We must stick to this 50-foot screen height for coming over the airfield boundary."

Pilot: "Why?"

Inspector: "In case there is a tall vehicle such as a double-deck bus on the road next to the end of the runway."

Pilot: "There are no double-deck buses in Orkney and on this island there are only 17 tractors and 8 cars!"

. . . . Silence.

Inspector: "What is the increment to runway roll taking off from long grass?"

And so on and on it went! Nothing, it seemed, was right. After the inspectors had finished the "tour" and had left the aircraft, one of them happened to turn around and look back at the plane. His jaw dropped perceptibly and for several seconds he stared in obvious disbelief at what he had just left. The Islander now wasn't only "travel stained," it looked for all the world like an animated pile of *sharne*!

"And what," asked the inspector sarcastically, "is the increment for the excrement?"

* * *

One more WHITSUNTIDE and Lufthansa Captain Rudolf Braunburg would have flown non-stop to Outer Mongolia! (Lutfhansa Photo)

Too Much Is Too Much!

Loganair in the Orkney Islands doesn't have the only pilots who have flown backwards. Pilots of Lufthansa, the German airline, also have demonstrated the art of flying in reverse, though not from a meteorological standpoint. Pilots of Loganair are able to accomplish this feat with the aid of Orkney's consistently gale-like winds. The following Lufthansa pilots performed it by the cooperation—or *un*-cooperation—of the element of time—the International Date Line. In fact, according to Captain Rudolf Braunburg, who relates the story, they even flew ahead of themselves, resulting in the whole business becoming just too much of a good thing!

It all began when Captain Braunburg and his crew landed "down under." "It's a nice place to be, really," he opined, "but to be in the southern hemisphere instead of Holland today of all days? Is that really necessary? It's *Christmas*!"

✈ **Lufthansa**

Things did indeed look bleak for the Lufthansa crew who would not be able to celebrate their style of Christmas at home; in fact, the outlook seemed anything but merry. What ensued can best be told by Captain Braunburg.

"Instead of flying back from Djakarta via Bankok and Karachi on the 20th of December, we were ordered to Sydney on an emigrants' chartered flight. Inscrutable are the ideas of the big boss and his airline company. Okay, okay—we're not complaining, and we arrived at Sydney in the evening of the 20th, red-eyed from loss of sleep, with a buzz in the ears and an exceedingly dry throat. Sweating like fury, we arrived at Menzies Hotel. It's 91 degrees and back in Deutschland they're now cutting the silver-tip fir in the snow-blanketed woods.

"We were just about to go to bed, doggone tired as we were, when the station chief, a certain Hoffmann, called to tell us he knew how miserable one felt so far away from home at Yuletide, and he fully understood. He knew also where we were to fly during the days following. He didn't know precisely where, but it sure wouldn't be Germany!

"What exactly did he want?

"Well, he had organized for the crew a lovely, genuine German Christmas celebration, with home-made cookies. His wife was preparing the dinner and in three-quarters of an hour he would drive up. Although admittedly the 20th of December was a bit early for Christmas, we did not know where we would be for the days to come. So back we got into our clothes and off we went for a German Christmas party.

"While we were on our way, we saw an interesting sight. Many bathers were going to some moonlight beach near Sydney; the car radio forecast a hot spell for Christmas Eve.

"The party starts and it exceeds all expectations.

"Frau Hoffmann, born at Aix-la-Chapalle, serves typical German Christmas cookies and specialties from her hometown (known as 'Aachener Printen')—all home-made!

"Isn't it a lovely surprise? The kids are singing 'In dulce jubilo' in the guests' honor. Everyone raises his glass with negus to everyone else. There's a smell of almonds, cinnamon and hazelnut—and outside sweating masses are rolling by towards the harbor ferry. With a solemn gesture, a fir is getting exposed to the admiring views of all of us, flown in from Germany for that very purpose. Herr Hoffmann steps to the refrigerator and takes out a frozen box containing genuine beeswax candles from Germany. Later in the evening they got bent nevertheless, but at that time we were singing the old German Christmas carols in somewhat high spirits, but always the first stanzas only.

"It was really a charming courtesy of the Hoffmann family, we decided unanimously, tired as we were.

"On the next day we were flying over the Pacific Ocean with its atolls and reefs, approaching Noumea.

"On the 21st—it was actually nearly the 22nd—we landed in New Caledonia as we had been flying towards the International Date Line.

"Although it was in the small hours of the morning (or somewhat late, if you prefer), a certain Barg and his family had stayed up and were awaiting us. He knew how miserable one felt far away from home at Christmas, and he knew where we were to fly next—and it sure wouldn't be Germany!

"So at five in the morning we arrived at the scene of the second German Christmas party. Some celebrating can never do any harm; the negus is really excellent and this time it's spiced with lots of clove and nutmeg. Frau Barg, raised partly in Holland and partly on Java, serves cookies and a genuine, although somewhat tough, Dutch specialty called Tai-Tai. The kids are singing German Christmas carols and a Dutch carol, 'Zie de maan schynt door de bomen,' although it's really a St.

Nicholas carol. There's a smell of almonds, cinnamon and hazelnut—and outside on the beach early surfboarders dare their first attempts. A rose-red tropical sun is rising. Tenderly we are singing the old carol, 'Es ist ein Ros entsprungen.' Stewardess Bela now even knows the second stanza.

"After these festivities we well deserved one-and-a-half days of rest and sleep. In the evening on the beach, when we had our sleep out and the Polynesians went to bed, our cabin cook, Karlheinz, complained of his senses being affected by hallucinations—the surf would smell of punch! Such a reaction is unreasonably premature and our purserette Schonhals classifies her colleague as 'unfit for any Christmas celebrations.'

"On the afternoon of December 23 we were flying back to Singapore with a stop-over at Port Darwin. The co-pilot expressed his hope that perhaps we would be back in Germany on Christmas in spite of all this; yet he's attracting a rather weak applause.

"At Darwin the air temperature on the runway is 106 degrees. It's early in the evening. It's all right though; after all, we'll take off again in an hour, sighs Bela. She's still sighing four and a half hours later as an important hydraulic line had failed which wasn't supposed to fail—not that one! For the duration of the repair work the station chief, a kind old guy named Regensburg, took us to a swiftly improvised more family-type Christmas party. He knew how one felt when being so far away from home at Yuletide. We are attempting to feel that way and are nodding enthusiastically. In Germany a gentleman keeps silent.

"While the obligatory hymns and carols are being sung solemnly, Christmas fruit loaves (raised cake with black currants, raisins, almonds, candied lemon and orange peel for the most important ingredients), roast goose and other Christmas surprises are served. Karlheinz, who's eating a Christmas dish heartily for the third time, relatively often retires to the restroom while records of Christmas choirs are being played

152

and the host's granddaughter is reciting Christmas poems.

"When Stewardess Bela is again offered chocolate pretzels from the famous one-kilo box, she burst out laughing hysterically. Kind old Herr Regensburg knows the tropical frenzy and is comforting her; and the only medicine is: eat heartily, kid! Bela is looking at him unhappily.

"Five and a half hours later we took off over the mangrove swamps of the bay. Perhaps we still can manage to be back in Germany by Christmas. The co-pilot keeps hoping, but Purserette Schonhals says that she couldn't stand many more Christmases.

"The cabin cook enters the cockpit and requests that the reading candles above the seats be blown out. There was a terrible smell of wax; but this, of course, exceeds by far harmless hallucinations!

"In Singapore we sneaked out of the airport building through a side entrance and hired commercial taxies to take us to the hotel. On a cross-road, however, the station chief caught us and took us to a genuine German Christmas celebration. This would be something really new for a change because each of us certainly had been on one of those foolish modern parties before. No, sir—his would be a celebration all homely and un- pretentious. Cabin Cook Karlheinz all of a sudden is drum- ming a beat rhythm on the seats and starts bawling, 'Get run- ning, ye shepherds.' Bela is having a silent crying fit, and the flight engineer is trying in vain to short-circuit the bus' ignition system.

"In the well decorated apartment we found the, by now, familiar utensils designed to generate the typical German Christmas mood; and everything was even more beautiful than anything previous. When the official party was over, we jointly apologized for the co-pilot and stewardess Regine Raff. The co-pilot had had a depressive fit and wrecked the Christmas tree, while Regine had modeled Easter bunnies from candle butts.

"The next morning we were having an emergency meeting

and found out it isn't even Christmas Eve! It's still ahead of us as we were to fly towards the West, away from the Date Line: in Bangkok, Delhi, Karachi. But not more than three times, says Regine, humming a song and belching unashamedly. We sent out a telex to all stations in the Far, Middle and Near East: REQUEST CANX ANY XMAS PARTY UPON ARR DUE EXCEED PARTYDUTYTIME OF STRESSED CREW.

"We paid one Singapore dollar because Karlheinz had ignited an angel made from tinsel that was decorating the telex room, and Regine had scribbled on the wall: STILL 144 DAYS TO GO TILL WHITSUNTIDE.

"Purserette Schonhals finally found the most appropriate solution. We're going to swap jobs, she cried happily, with a crew coming in from Germany sad as can be, and let them fly back to Germany happily and take over their flight to Tahiti. Thus, Schonhals is telling us, we'll spend Christmas Eve in the stratosphere over the Timor Sea and when we touch down, it will be the 25th of December in Sydney for we'll fly towards the East—towards the Date Line!

"And that's the reason why all of us got a laudatory letter from the airline company for our kind offer (obligingness) towards the other crew.

"But what we sadly forgot to take into account was—since we had to cross the Date Line several times between Sydney and Tahiti, we were given the "benefit" of *five* New Year's Eve parties!"

* * *

154

An Alpine LunAIRtic?

Several years ago a calendar cartoon by cartoonist Clyde Lamb depicted an airplane flying past a mountain peak with a mountain goat hanging from the plane's landing gear by its horns. The co-pilot was saying to the pilot: "Circle back, Joe—I thought I saw a mountain goat on that last peak!"

In terms of one scheduled European airline this isn't as far-fetched as it seems, other than the fact that landing gears no longer sport axles on which mountain goats can become entangled.

We speak of Air-Alpes, the airline created by Martin Ziegler, Europe's—if not the world's—premier glacier pilot. Now you know, and we know, that if ever an airline would proclaim its immediate destination as a glacier high in the Alps, we would unhesitatingly switch our reservations to another supposedly far saner line faster than one could say Ed-

AIR ALPES founder and president, Michael Ziegler, noted glacier pilot and mountain guide.
(Jean Perard Photo)

die Rickenbacker.

In Air-Alpes case, however, we would quite likely reconsider because, as ridiculous as it may sound, Air-Alpes' first stop *is* on a glacier high in the Alps and those ticketed for a flight on this line know for sure that is exactly where they will wind up—safe and sound!

As a bonafide scheduled air service between several European cities and two dozen or more glacial landing areas known as altiports, Air-Alpes has to be one of the world's most oddball air services.

The whole idea of this high-landing airline was conceived by Ziegler's agile brain a dozen or more years ago. Noting winter sports fans flocking to Alpine snowfields from the four corners of the earth, it was his contention that these snow bunnies and snow bucks might relish getting to their respective play areas the quickest and easiest way possible and, of course, his wheel-

156

AIR ALPES

and-ski-equipped Piper Cub was the obvious answer, especially since he had already attained widespread recognition for his prowess in landing and taking off from high, steep glaciers and mountain snowfields.

Somehow, though, the majority of these snow bucks and bunnies weren't exactly agog over landing on steep Alpine snowfields in an airplane—especially one as fragile-looking as Ziegler's, and continued getting to their play areas by other tried and true methods. Nevertheless Ziegler was not one who would easily toss in the towel, so to speak. In fact his stubbornness was outdone only by his mountain flying ability and recreationists soon discovered that Ziegler always managed to come back from each Alpine flight he made. That made some semblance of sense to them and business rapidly improved. Soon he was not only hauling capacity loads to these high altiports, but in addition was flying skiers from one high snowfield to another.

As Ziegler's fame spread, so, too, did his Air-Alpes grow. Today it operates a fleet of 21 aircraft, most of them S.T.O.L.'s (short take-off and landing) of from 8- to 19-passenger capacity capable of landing equally well in cities, mountains or on glaciers. Air-Alpes, too, may take credit for having constructed more than 25 altiports, some with as much as 30% slope! The company at this writing carries upwards of

AIR ALPES airliner deposits a load of snow devotees on one of its altiports.   (Jean Perard Photo)

50,000 passengers a year and boasts a company staff of 150.

Although Ziegler has become a pilot of considerable note in the playlands of the Alps, he clearly recalls when such recognition was not accorded him by at least one person.

It happened one unprofitable day in 1962, back when that lowly Piper Cub was the sole piece of Air-Alpes' flying equipment. A howling blizzard had not only blanketed the Alps with heavy snow, but with heavy fog as well since, in Alpine meteorology, each go hand-in-hand. The result was zero passengers, zero visibility, and a forced overnight altiport stay for Ziegler.

It was Ziegler's practice when grounded on an altiport by such storms to bury his Cub's skis and wheels in a hole,

158

The Piper Cub that started it all shown nesting in its "snow anchorage."
(Air Alpes Photo)

bolstering this highly-engineered anchorage with well-tamped snow. After this particularly wild blizzard, however, Ziegler questioned the adequacy of such minor precautions. It therefore was with considerable apprehension that, with broom and shovel, he fought his way out to the altiport from a small shelter cabin nearby.

The altiport by now was completely covered with deep snowdrifts, and, to make matters worse, storm-generated fog hampered his visibility. It was with some difficulty that he arrived at the spot where he thought he had left his plane, only to find his fears confirmed. The plane had gone "over the hill" and left not the slightest hint as to which direction it had taken. Existing conditions certainly did not give him any desire to yodel. All he could do now was to wade through the drifts, poking here and there with his shovel hoping for a lucky strike.

He was still at his seemingly hopeless task two hours later when suddenly an apparently hardy skier emerged through the mist, presumably village bound. As the skier approached he saw it was a young woman. Thinking she just may have spotted the Cub along the line of her descent, he waved a greeting at the young skiatrix and hopefully called, "Have you seen my plane somewhere around here?"

The pretty femme came to a halt, stared at him for a full minute in open-mouthed horror and then, with a shriek of terror, sped off on her skis in a great swirl of snow as though the devil himself were after her! It was obvious she knew nothing of his flight operations in the Alps and had taken him for either a completely mad man or a misplaced abominable snowman of Himalayan renown.

He continued to probe about, all the while hoping he would meet another skier who would consider him as being of sound mind and who just might have seen the aircraft. No one else appeared.

At the end of the third hour, just as Ziegler figured his wing-ed partner had taken off on a one-way pilotless sightseeing hop, leaving him holding the company "bag," he spotted a slight protrusion through one of the drifts. It was the Cub, un-harmed but so embedded in ice and snow it took him three days to extricate it, and all the while he hoped the pretty skier would return so he could prove he was in possession of all his faculties, but no such luck.

The Air-Alpes of today has far outgrown buried Cubs and pilots who strike terror into the hearts of skiing mademoiselles. Instead it is a fine, ever-growing service serving the needs of those myriad snow bunnies and snow bucks.

* * *

Heave Ho!

How to literally get "teeth" into a situation is an incident recalled by Captain Joe E. Kimm of Northwest Airlines, said situation occurring during the "Tin Goose" (Ford tri-motor) and "pre-stewardii" days of air transport. This was in 1931 when airline flying was still a novel method of transportation attracting none but the airminded, the light-headed, or those prone to exult in appearing brave to the rest of the "cowardly" world.

Among the so-called advantages the airlines had to offer in those days, aside from getting the passenger to his or her destination somewhat faster than ground methods, were an eagle's-eye view of the countryside, free box lunches, coffee and water from thermos containers and uncontaminated fresh air obtainable by the simple expedient of opening the sliding glass windows, admissible in those days of low flight and 90-

Co-author Ann Bohrer, pioneer Pacific Northwest flyeress, with Northwest Airlines Captains Joe Kimm (center) and L. S. DeLong (right) on occasion of anniversary flight of one of NWA's early Ford tri-motors.(Ackroyd Photo)

1928 Ford tri-motor.

100 m.p.h. speeds. Cruising altitude was rarely above 2,000 feet and mostly between 500 and 1,000 feet. The reasons for this on-deck flying were that the engines were not supercharged and, therefore, performed with more power at lower altitudes; instrument flying had not as yet been developed, and the weather-forecasting of the day was not exactly tailored to the particular needs of airline flight. Consequently all flights had to be made under contact conditions with whatever weather information it was possible to glean by long-distance calls ahead to towns along the route.

This low flying, or "hedge-hopping" as it was known among fliers, made each trip a bumpy—or turbulent—one and a few of the less hardy passengers would wind up with a bad case of airsickness. This accounted for the neatly folded paper bag in the pocket of each passenger's seat, along with chewing gum and a wad of cotton to keep the ears from popping.

In the circumstances, the co-pilots naturally became very familiar with the paper-bag routine and developed a speed and dexterity in getting rid of the "offending material" adequately enough to meet most situations. There was one co-pilot, however, who became a mite too proficient in the promptness with which he disposed of paper bags. That co-pilot was a fellow named Bert Ritchie, later to become a Minneapolis-based captain.

This revoltin' development, to snatch a phrase from a television show, happened on a run from Chicago to the Twin Cities and involved one of the passengers—an elderly and very dignified sister of the Chairman of the Board who had flown to Chicago to obtain dentures without her family's knowledge. The subterfuge was clearly one of pride as it was far from her desire to let it be known, even to her family, that she had reached the denture stage although it was obvious to everyone that the bloom of youth had long since gone AWOL. Now as she winged back home very pleased with her "store-boughten" teeth, she undoubtedly congratulated herself upon employing such a clever ruse with which to hoodwink her family and friends.

It was shortly after they had left Chicago that the air waves became so choppy the plane was going up and down in fast elevator style and, in the same instant, flipping to one side and the other not unlike a Coney Island thrill ride. Riding this bucking aerial bronc soon made most of the passengers turn various shades of green, including the very proud sister of the Board Chairman. Bert, therefore, was kept on the hop passing out paper sacks and then getting rid of them as quickly as possible before the bottoms fell out. The customary "getting rid of" process was to throw out of the cabin door anything which wasn't needed inside in the belief that it was blown to little bits, anyway, and never reached the ground, and, as stated before, Bert had become a master at this disposal technique and rolicking down the aisle of a pitching ship didn't slow him down one little bit.

So it was that fortunately, or unfortunately as it turned out, Bert was a veritable Johnny-on-the-spot with a bag when the owner of the new false teeth became violently ill. After she had used the bag, he handed her a fresh one and quickly tossed the used one out of the door.

Eventually the woman felt well enough to take an interest in living but not for long as she soon got the shock of her life—and became ill all over again. She discovered her new teeth were missing—and she knew exactly where they were: in

164

the paper bag which the co-pilot had so gingerly tossed out into space! So, as it turned out, her secret was no secret any more and, without doubt, at some later date, some unsuspecting Midwest farmer is going to encounter a slightly beat-up set of false choppers leering up at him!

* * *

Flying wasn't always the serene mode of transportation it is today. As indicated in previous episodes, before the days of pressurized aircraft it was necessary to fly at low altitudes where the air was often rough, as well as sultry, on muggy summer days. It therefore was not unusual for passengers to become airsick even on short flights. To compensate for any resulting regurgitation, there was provided for each passenger, the tube-like carton which superceded the earlier paper bag and which could be sealed off with a cap after use. Although airsickness in itself is not a laughing matter, the results, as witnessed by Captain R. John Wisda of United Air Lines, sometimes took on a humorous aspect.

For instance, one particularly hot, rough day he noted one of his passengers gradually succumbing to the buckings of the DC-3. Moisture began forming on his brow and his lips and face were paling slowly to that tell-tale shade of green. Before long he reached for the burp-cup. The dew on the passenger's face increased and the green hue deepened noticeably. Finally in one agonizing, gasping retch, he leaned over the cup.

The passenger may have felt better afterward but he certainly didn't look it—and for good reason. He had failed to remove the lid on the cup!

* * *

On another particularly hot, rough trip at low altitudes, the stewardess on Captain Wisda's flight was doing a heroic job of tending the needs of many ill-feeling passengers. In the rolling, pitching airplane she would bounce up and down the aisle like a yo-yo, passing out damp towels, comforting frantic passengers and distributing burp-cups, both new and used. On one of her many trips about half way up the aisle, a distressed little old lady tugged at her sleeve. The stewardess knew at a glance that the woman's lunch would soon be en route up. Quickly she procured a burp-cup, removed the lid and held it before the woman—and just in time!

The last thought in the minds of either of the women was that the receptacle could be defective. But it was! The bottom was gone—and from all appearances so was the passenger's dress!

* * *

13

Forced Landings

While not entirely a thing of the past, forced landings by airliners are now almost non-existent. In earlier air transport years, however, one could expect a periodic forced landing. Contributing causes were weather, engine trouble or, on rare occasions, fire.

Following are several such incidents, all with happy endings:

When commercial airlines were still in their infancy, they referred to their captains and first officers as pilots and co-pilots. Mal Freeburg was one of these early-day captains and among his best remembered experiences while flying for Northwest Airlines, now known as Northwest Orient Airlines, are the following two, both of which involved unheralded landings from which he miraculously walked away. Strangely enough this is not what he remembers most about the incidents. It was the complete indifference of the Wisconsin

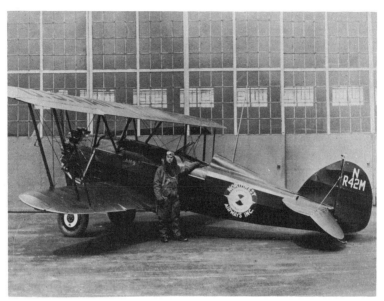

NWA Waco "Taperwing", pilot, Mal Freeburg.

farmer that stamped itself so indelibly upon his memory. Such lack of interest was all the more amazing since in those early days of aviation, even a straight-flying plane aroused the curiosity of most people. A plane crash was a cinch to bring out the entire populace from miles around.

The first Wisconsin episode occurred in 1930 when he was flying both as an airmail and passenger pilot for Northwest. He had taken off from Chicago at 11:30 p.m. in a taper-wing Waco carrying mail only. The temperature at the time was 35° above. Over Sparta, Wisconsin he encountered an unexpected drop to 40° below. The Wright J6 engine, not being cowled for this sort of meteorological caper, began stuttering like a bashful school boy and about ten minutes later, quit completely. Mal at first thought the power failure was due to the engine's swallowing an intake valve but later found it was because of the extreme temperature change.

From his 7,000-foot perch, he noticed a lone light about five miles ahead. In the inky blackness of the night, this glow was

168

Chief pilot Mal Freeburg seated at Link recorder in Northwest Airlines' Link Trainer station.

the "lamp in the window" bidding him welcome. He nosed in the direction of the light, hoping there would be a spot into which he could at least pancake. When directly over the light, he pulled a flare and proceeded to spiral rapidly in its path. Somehow or other as they neared the ground, he and the flare parted company, it disappearing down one side of a hill and he going down the other. Now that his guiding light was gone, he felt like a kid lost in a dense forest. His throat was tight and dry and his hands were trembling but he told himself this was no time for panic. Leaning far over the side of the cockpit, he desperately tried to penetrate the darkness to see what lay directly ahead. As he neared the ground he saw it was blanketed in snow. The ground appeared level enough but, of course, he had no way of telling just what lay under the snow or how deep it was. Since there appeared to be no obstacles in his immediate path except the light several hundred feet ahead, he took a deep breath and hauled back on the stick, hoping the snow was deep enough to "brake" his run but not nose him over. The ship sank into about two feet of the soft blanket and rolled to a stop within 200 feet of the light. As he was right side up and uninjured, he felt he had really made a top-notch bull's-eye landing.

His relief in getting down safely was so great he could but lean back in the cockpit with closed eyes. As he breathed deeply of the cold Wisconsin night air, he realized he was shaking like a leaf.

It was only then he noted the light was moving. Startled, he watched it for a few seconds and saw it was a lantern in the hands of a farmer who, he later learned, had been out to the barn caring for some sick stock. Mal's first reaction was to hop out of the ship and call to the farmer but he knew his quaking legs would fold under him like a camp stool. Dumbfoundedly he watched the light pass him, proceed to the farmhouse and go inside. Shortly the light went out. He was unable to believe his eyes. The man had ignored him completely! If he had not seen the glare of the flare and the ship descend against the whiteness of the snow, surely he must have heard the swoosh of the plane as it came in for a landing almost on top of him!

As soon as Mal dared to walk, he went to the house and rapped. The light was shortly re-lighted and the farmer came to the door. Before Mal could utter a word, the man asked, "Oh, did you want something?" The asininity of the question so amazed Mal that for a moment he was speechless. After he explained what had occurred, he was hospitably invited inside. The farmer then awakened the rest of his family and had one of his sons drive Mal and the mail 19 miles to the nearest town. Upon their return, a breakfast, which would have done justice to a starving logger, awaited them. To this day Mal maintains it was the best breakfast he had ever eaten. During this repast the farmer explained he thought the flare was merely another ship on fire and that Mal had landed to help the unfortunate pilot. Considering it none of his business, he had gone back to bed.

* * *

170

Two years later in 1932 Freeburg had his second forced landing in Wisconsin which once more was to introduce him to the incredible indifference of the Wisconsin farmer.

He was on a routine Northwest Airlines flight from Minneapolis to Chicago in a Ford tri-motor with mail again his only cargo. As he was nearing Wabasha, Wisconsin, the prop blade suddenly broke at the hub and, in leaving, sliced off approximately 13 feet of the left wing tip. This unbalanced condition was such that the left outboard Pratt & Whitney Hornet engine immediately shook loose from its mount. The old "tin goose" heaved to like a drunken sailor. Looking over the side, Mal gasped at what he saw. In tearing away, the engine had lodged in the left landing gear V as though quite reluctant to part company with his ship, while the remaining prop blade had neatly sliced off the left landing wheel. Now wasn't that just ducky, he asked himself. What a predicament to be in. The only thing that seemed to be intact as yet was himself, but the way he was shaking he wasn't any too sure how long *he* would hold together.

The first thing on the flight agenda would be to try to shake the engine free. In the distance, the Mississippi River, glimmering in the sun, appeared to be ideal for this purpose. Taking careful aim, he headed for the water. This time, however, his bombing ability left much to be desired. He was "off target" by at least three miles. Meanwhile he and Old Mother Earth were becoming chummier by the minute and he knew he had to shake himself loose of that clinging power plant in no time flat—or else. There was considerable open country below, so he began to put the ship through a mad rock and roll routine. He recalls wondering dryly which was shaking the more—he or the ship. In what seemed an eternity, he finally dislodged the engine and headed for the nearest emergency field. He prayed fervently as he sank toward it that he could keep the ship right side up when making his one-wheel landing so as not to entirely tear off the left wing. Apparently his luck hadn't completely deserted him because, other than a sharp jolt when the plane dropped on the landing gear V, it was a fair landing. In fact, since he walked away from it, it was perfect!

He telephoned his St. Paul headquarters for another plane to continue the flight, and while waiting for the ship, borrowed a car from one of the gathered curious to find where the engine had landed. He drove to where he thought it might be but it was nowhere about. After resorting to a farm to farm check in the immediate vicinity, he was finally directed to one where he found the owner shingling the roof of a chicken house. He asked the farmer if he had seen an airplane engine fall. The man, his mouth full of nails, flicked his eyes over Mal and continued to hammer away. At first Mal thought he had not heard the question. Just as he was about to repeat it, the farmer, without missing a hammer stroke, nodded his head in an easterly direction. Mal stared at the man. In memory he saw another farmer with lantern in hand, suffused in light and indifference. Mal looked at the farmer on the roof. Instead of a lantern, there was a hammer in his hand and nails in his mouth but there he was clothed in the same cloak of indifference. Mal opened his mouth to make some final comment but so far as this shingler was concerned, Mal was non-existent. He could have gotten more attention from one of the cackling residents of the hen house. That he miraculously survived what was obviously a most harrowing experience seemed to be, as in the Sparta case, none of this Wisconsinite's business.

Turning on his heel, Mal walked in the direction indicated by the man's head. There, a mere 100 feet from where the man was working, he found the engine buried 10 feet in the ground! The farmer had been on the roof when the engine had fallen but obviously had not swallowed a nail or missed a beat with his hammer.

Although Mal, through the years, has been able to cope with the idiosyncracies of airplanes and airplane engines, he has yet to fathom the indifference of the Wisconsin farmer.

* * *

172

Why should a tank running dry, a choking co-pilot or a passenger giving birth to a baby shake up a pilot? But when it all happens at once, as it did to United Air Lines Captain Frank Swaim, it's a horse of a different hue!

Captain Frank L. Swaim recalls a flight which left him with rather wobbly underpinnings. He still recalls this as his *triple threat* flight and it happened on a United Air Lines run between Omaha and Denver and began at the former city with seemingly two strikes against him. First, on this flight he had a spanking-new co-pilot which in itself can be somewhat unnerving for a captain as he can't help but wonder about an unfamiliar partner sitting beside him. It was a foregone conclusion, of course, that the man was an expert pilot or he would not have been employed in the first place but there was that thing, precision. In the control room it is as much a paramount factor in the achievement of success as in the roaring mechanical horses out front. Compatability, or team work, therefore, means a great deal and in this regard Swaim could only hope this would be just such an alliance.

The second more or less unnerving note was the pregnant woman who boarded the plane at Omaha. It was obvious the stork wasn't too far off; in fact Swaim feared the bird might even now be bucking his slipstream.

Captain Swaim was at the controls as they left Omaha. The ship was a Douglas DC-3. While en route, he operated the engines on an alternate fuel tank, eventually changing back to the regular main tanks, which was normal procedure for using extra fuel loads, but one which required close monitoring.

The co-pilot, meanwhile, experienced an inner gnawing familiar to most pilots—and they all come hungry—which suggested his "tank" also could use a bit of refueling and since Swaim was at the controls, he figured this was an ideal time to "fill 'er up!"

Hauling out his lunch, which included a flavorsome fresh peach for dessert, he commenced to gratify the inner man. Just as he was in the midst of savoring the luscious fruit, a red light flashed and a bell began to ring for attention. This indicated that all was not exactly Kosher, so to speak; in fact, what it meant was the gas tank was totally dry.

This danger signal so startled the new eager beaver co-pilot that he swallowed the peach seed which lodged at a point midway between his mouth and stomach. At this precise moment, as Swaim was attempting to decide which of the two serious conditions required priority consideration, the stewardess rushed forward with further upsetting news. The long-legged bird was "rounding the last pylon!" And there sat the co-pilot choking into a purplish hue to the accompaniment of the flashing red light and ringing bell. Swaim didn't waste precious minutes wondering what to do first. So far as he was concerned, Mother Nature had just decided for him. He'd had it!

While lustily thumping the sputtering co-pilot on the back, Swaim nosed the plane down to an unheralded landing at North Platte, Nebraska—just a couple of laps, or flaps, ahead of the stork!

Although the triple threat was now well in hand, Swaim suffered a bad case of the heebie-jeebies for at least a full week thereafter.

* * *

A few years back if you wanted to get away from it all, Captain C. J. Stropes of United Air Lines could have informed you of just the right spot for seclusion—Hanksville, Utah, 125 miles southwest of Grand Junction. At that time, the nearest paved road was 55 miles north, the nearest electric lights and telephone were at Greenriver, Utah, 65 miles distant. The population was about a hundred people, plus a few yapping dogs and cackling chickens—and a record number of prairie dogs.

With the advent of the four-engined airliner, a more modern touch was brought to this part of the country, although it was more for the benefit of the airlines than the town's populace. As a safety measure, the airlines decided to construct a secondary field along their regular route; therefore an airway was laid out between Las Vegas and Denver, after which the CAA put in a radio station and graded a 6,000-foot strip out of the mesquite brush and prairie dog mounds. This emergency field amid the prairie varmints was soon to be a welcome sight for the crew of a United Air Liner on the Denver-Los Angeles run.

It was the morning flight of the day the following incident occurred. Since it was also ham 'n' egg time, hunger pangs were nipping Captain Stropes' innards and he was eagerly looking forward to his morning java and its accompaniments. With a visibility of 90 miles, he transferred the controls to automatic pilot and turned to his breakfast.

In the midst of the morning repast, the warning light for No. 2 engine flashed, indicating trouble. The necessary feathering was promptly accomplished and the carbon dioxide extinguisher fired into the engine. The light went out. In a few seconds, Los Angeles had moved 20 minutes further away;

however it was no great problem to manage a DC-6 on three engines. Stropes continued eating.

Two minutes later the warning light for engine No. 3 came on. First Officer Ed Osterling took a quick look out the window and confirmed there was a fire. Came a repeat performance of feathering and firing of extinguisher, and although this did the trick, Stopes had no hopes of arriving at Los Angeles. The problem that had caused two fires in rapid succession might cause others and Stopes wasn't taking any chances. Hanksville was just 30 minutes ahead.

Tossing the remnants of his breakfast toward Flight Engineer Clancy Tightener, Stropes took over the controls from the automatic pilot. It now was a case of get the airplane on the ground. Hanksville, here we come!

United Air Lines was advised by radio of the decision to land, and the CAA station at Hanksville also was alerted. In an east-bound DC-6, Captain E. E. Hitch had caught the radioed message and interrupted his flight to orbit the descending liner. Not until Stropes had brought his crippled aircraft safely down on the dirt strip, did Hitch resume his schedule.

Stropes taxied the big craft to the CAA building and cut the two remaining engines. A ladder was placed against the door and the passengers gingerly filed down. As they surveyed the bleak, drouth-browned mesas, one passenger turned to the CAA operator.

"Where," asked he, "is the nearest phone?" He apparently wanted to notify friends or relatives that although he was down, he was not out.

The operator, with passive expression, led the passenger around the tail of the plane and stopped. The puzzled passenger looked at the operator. The latter, pointing up a dusty, dirt trace, replied, "Right up that road—65 miles!"

* * *

Out of Finnair's history comes the story of an old Junkers Ju-52 flying from Turku to Stockholm and losing its middle

Finnair Captain Helge Laitinen knows difficulties—and French horn players, too, apparently!   (Finnair Photo)

Finnair Junker JU-52 fly better on 3 engines.

engine which fell into the sea. This naturally had the effect of making the plane tail-heavy instantaneously but Captain "Helge" Laitinen nevertheless managed to return to Turku on his two remaining engines.

Upon landing one of the passengers asked Helge whether it hadn't been awfully difficult to fly with only two engines.

"No," tossed off Helge, "that's not so difficult. What I'd call difficult would be a French horn player blowing his horn straight and then sucking it back into shape again!"

* * *

Getting Nowhere Fast!

With all the comforts of today's modern airliners and their many other attractions—both gastronomic and visual, flying can be a most relaxing mode of travel. Ordinary cares of the day can dissolve into nothingness as one rests against the soft confines of the reclining chairs, partaking of a gourmet meal or sipping a refreshing beverage. Many passengers can relax to the extent of luxuriating in a nap during the entire trip and awaken thoroughly refreshed. One case in point, however, would have turned out better had the passenger never entered dreamland. The ensuing events were not only embarrassing to the passenger but had him believing he was having a nightmare—all of which certainly was not conducive to converting a patron of the rails to one of the sky lanes. This sad state of affairs occurred in 1933 and Zay Smith of United Air Lines tells the story:

"A Chicago man who had never flown before—in fact had never even been in the terminal at Chicago—had gone to New York on the train but was suddenly recalled to Chicago and so, although he hated it, he took a plane. He was asleep when the ship began its descent to Cleveland and when the stewardess awakened him to ask if he wished to walk around during the time they would be on the ground, he declined grumpily and went back to sleep after learning that the estimated time of arrival in Chicago was 5:00 p.m.

"After leaving Cleveland word was received that Chicago had socked in solid with fog and visibility was zero-zero so the flight was ordered back to Cleveland. The stewardess, remembering how unpleasant this particular Chicago passenger had been when she had awakened him before, said nothing to him when she noticed that he had awakened himself just before landing.

"He glanced at his watch. It was a few minutes before 5:00 p.m. As soon as the door was opened he was the first one out. He rushed into the terminal and into a telephone booth. He dialed his home phone number. As soon as the receiver was lifted, he said, 'I'm at the airport, dear. I'll take a cab and be home in a few minutes.'

" 'You must have the wrong number,' said the voice on the other end. 'What number do you want?'

" 'Is this 234-5678?' he shouted.

" 'Yes, it is. Who do you want?'

" 'I want my wife. Who is this anyway?'

" 'Well, your wife is not here!' said she emphatically and hung up.

"Furious, he dialed the number again.

" 'Oh, *you* again! Why don't you look up the number you want and stop bothering me?'

" 'Look, lady, I don't know what you're doing in my house and for your information I have been paying the phone bill on that number for 20 years and I don't need to look it up!'

"By now the woman was sure he was some kind of nut so

simply hung up the receiver.

"Thoroughly frustrated, the Chicagoan staggered out of the booth and went up to the ticket agent. 'They tell me I don't know my own phone number. Am I dreaming? Are *you* going to tell me I didn't just arrive in that plane from Cleveland?'

" 'Yes, you did arrive on it because I saw you rush in.'

" 'Are you going to tell me I'm not in Chicago?'

" 'Well, no sir. You are *not* in Chicago.'

" 'Then where in the hell *am* I?'

" 'You're in Cleveland.'

" 'Like *hell* I am! Has the whole world gone crazy? I left Cleveland two hours ago!' "

* * *

As the foregoing story proves, sometimes it doesn't pay *not* to get up! Further evidence to substantiate this fact is in the following story which went the rounds about 1940 when United Air Lines was flying sleepers. Again Zay Smith tells it:

"After leaving Chicago westbound a passenger told the stewardess that he wished to be awakened as late as possible in order to deplane in Salt Lake City. 'I'm a very sound sleeper and may protest and may even go back to sleep. Regardless of what I say or do, be sure to get me off!'

"The stewardess noted that he was in seat 4 which corresponded to lower 4. The berths were made up before reaching Cheyenne and all passengers turned in. Our friend, noticing that upper 4 was empty and that the head room in lower 4 was restricted, chose upper 4 and promptly went to sleep.

"He slept so soundly that he did not even know when they landed at Cheyenne where another passenger got on. 'You are in upper 4,' the stewardess told him as he came aboard.

" 'I know,' he replied, 'I can find it—don't bother.'

"On finding his upper occupied and the lower empty, he crawled in without disturbing anyone, even the stewardess.

"When the plane landed in San Francisco the man in upper

181

4 was extremely irate. 'I told you to put me off in Salt Lake City regardless of my protests. I'm very angry with you!'

" 'Yes, sir, I see that you are angry,' replied the stewardess, 'but you are not half as angry as the man we dragged out of lower 4 and put off the plane at Salt Lake!' "

15

AIRnecdotes

From the word "go" in air transport—and that takes us back to the old airmail days—humorous or interesting happenings, always with happy endings, have far outstripped the unhappy ones. In previous chapters we've tried to categorize these delightful happenstances, but there were always some remaining that failed to fit into any specific category. What better way then, to bring our book to a landing, would there be than to present these left-over AIRnecdotes in this final chapter?

For instance, if the good citizens of the farming area between Kimball, Nebraska and Pine Bluffs, Wyoming, have ever wondered why a stewardess' uniform skirt came floating down out of the sky one day, here is the answer:

During World War II it was a standing rule of United Air Lines that the stewardess should always buzz the cockpit on

the inter-phone before entering. On one of the flights a stewardess came forward with a tray of hot chocolate without first announcing herself in accordance with the rules. The result was that she stumbled over a flight bag and spilled the chocolate all over the front of her uniform skirt. She complained so vociferously that the crew, overcome with kindheartedness, offered to clean her skirt if she would step into the baggage pit and remove same.

So she brought up some hot water and a towel, stepped into the baggage pit, removed her skirt and passed it up to the crew. They, in turn, cleaned it nicely and passed it back.

On went the dress, accompanied by gripe number two. The dress was now too wet and cold. So it was that the naturally-patient crew offered then to dry it for her. The only way this could be accomplished was to open the side window of the cockpit to create a breeze. But lo and behold! the suction carried the skirt out the window about the time the plane was midway between the aforementioned communities. Adding insult to injury, the stewardess was forced to get a "civilian" skirt out of her traveling bag and wear it for the remainder of the flight. Since the brightest of plaid skirts were the current rage, the chagrined stewardess was as conspicuous as a polar bear in the Sahara Desert for the remainder of the trip.

* * *

In pre-stewardess-school days it was the duty of the pilots to train new stewardesses assigned to their flights. On one of United Air Lines' flights First Officer Zay Smith tried to reassure a nervous girl on her first assignment. "I reminded her," said Smith, "that she knew more than the average passenger about flying, and that what a passenger needed was the assurance of a stewardess who seemed to be sure of herself.

"When we arrived in New York she told me that giving the passengers a positive answer instead of an 'I don't know' had done much for her morale.

"On the return flight one of the old captains was dead-heading back in civilian clothes. Neither had ever met but it was obvious to the veteran pilot that the girl was new. While flying through dense clouds with zero visibility he asked the neophite what their altitude was. Undaunted, she pulled out her fountain pen pocket flashlight, shined it out the window in the general direction of the ground and said with supreme confidence, '5,000 feet over Sunbury.'

"Later, when in the clear, the same veteran pilot asked the new stewardess the names of some towns far below represented by three small patches of lights. She glanced at the name plates of the crew on the cockpit door (Captain Stapleton, First Officer Zay Smith and Stewardess Ruth Bussey) and without hesitation replied, 'Stapletown, Smithville and Bussy Corners.' "

* * *

The old magnetic compasses used in early airmail days were often the source of snafu'd navigation.

A classic example years ago was the experience of an airmail pilot en route from New York to Cleveland. A crate of engine parts stowed in his mail pit deflected his magnetic compass 150 degrees.

Unaware of the error, he flew on through the murky night toward what he thought was Ohio. When he finally let down he was over the Atlantic Ocean. Mistaking the ocean for Lake Erie, he turned left. Spotting the New England shoreline, he

The post office department's De Havilland DH-4's Liberty engine-powered air mail planes, Circa 1918.

thought it was Ohio. He was still looking for Cleveland when, about midnight, he ran out of gas, landed and cracked up.

Uninjured, except for a bump on his noggin, he hiked to the nearest farm house and pounded on the door. A sleepy-eyed Connecticut Yankee opened the door.

"Where's Cleveland?" asked the pilot.

Half asleep the farmer gaped at the begoggled figure as though he were a lunatic.

"Cleveland's dead," he replied. "Hoover's president now"—and slammed the door.

* * *

Where farmer's daughters were concerned airplane pilots were never overly-trusted and, in the early days, were ever regarded through Jimmy Finlayson-type glares of obvious fierce suspicion (head thrown back, right eye closed in a scornful squint, left eyebrow raised impossibly high) by any farmer possessing a beautiful daughter, and whose misfortune it was to have an airmail pilot pick his farm for a forced landing.

This, of course, included pilots who would eventually develop into airline captains, such as—say—retired United

United Air Lines Captain Walter (Doc) Eefsen
knew farmers' daughters—but not as well as the
farmers knew pilots. (United Air Lines Photo)

Air Lines Captain Walter (Doc) Eefsen.

Eefsen, then a Varney Air Lines pilot, encountered just such a ludicrous situation while on an extra mail flight from Boise, Idaho to Salt Lake City.

To make a long story short, his engine konked and he landed—yep! on the farm of a farmer with a beautiful daughter!

Well, the farmer invited him to stay for dinner, and also to spend the night. When they sat down to dinner, the farmer informed Eefsen the women would eat later, referring, of course, to his wife and said beautiful daughter. At bedtime, Eefsen was shown to his room—by the farmer.

About 3:00 a.m., feeling the call of Nature, Eefsen donned

Finn-Air Captain Viekko Harmala

his trousers in order to "go" outside the farmhouse. You guessed it! The farmer, who apparently knew pilots, had securely locked Eefsen in his room. So now here was an airmail pilot who needed "to go" with no place "to go". However, being an astute individual, he pried open the window and did what any pilot-in-misery would do. Thereupon he returned to bed and fell into a fitful sleep.

Upon awakening, sure enough! the door had been unlocked allowing Eefsen to proceed to the kitchen for breakfast with one smug-looking farmer!

"Just goes to show," declares Eefsen ruefully, "what one must go through to become an airline captain!"

* * *

In Finland, as all over the world, pilots and air control staff personnel use hours of the clock to indicate positions of other aircraft and objects that might endanger a pilot in flight.

Finnair Captain Veikko Harmala recounts that on one occasion when Air Traffic Control advised them to look out for another aircraft at 10:30, his co-pilot seemed very perplexed. Finally he turned to Captain Harmala and asked:

"Do they mean local or Greenwich Mean Time?"

* * *

188

Hotels in which airline personnel were quartered quite often lent humor to situations.

There was a certain Chicago-based captain who was getting ragged and run-down looking. He was on a Chicago-New York schedule with a Cleveland stop. He would arrive in New York around ll:00 a.m. and would not have to report back for his return flight to Chicago until 9:00 p.m., technically plenty of time for sleep. The New York dispatcher was getting quite worried over the increasingly haggard appearance of the captain and reported his concern. After due inquiry and investigation it was discovered that (1) the captain had a room directly across the street from an apartment hotel noted for its exclusive female clientele, and (2) it was further discovered that one girl in particular, on the floor directly opposite, was doing her housework and other duties completely in the nude! In the interests of airline passenger safety and the captain's health, the layover rooms of that flight were soon changed!

* * *

MEMBER OF THE SWIRE GROUP

CATHAY PACIFIC

THE AIRLINE THAT KNOWS THE ORIENT BEST

At the Oriental Hotel in Kobe, Japan, where Cathay Pacific Airline crews spend the night after landing in Osaka, the room phones have a "Dial-a-directory" attachment which states "Dial 4 for Overseas Massage," and at the multi-story Tokyo Prince Hotel Cathay Pacific crews found a notice on each window ledge admonishing "Please do not leave out of the window."

* * *

Hotels weren't the problem during British Overseas Airways Corporation's pre-jet refueling stops in the Maritimes—Gander, Newfoundland and Goose Bay,

Jack Knight prepares to climb into his DH for the first night
air mail flight.

U.S. Mail De Havilland DH-4's, Liberty engine powered, first planes used in
transcontinental air mail service.

Labrador. It was food. Meals placed on board BOAC's planes at both refueling stops were catered at Gander and there was a time during BOAC's Constellation days when its flight personnel were constantly fighting to get the quality of the food upgraded. It so happened that, at the time, the catering officer at Gander possessed the unlikely name of Sid Duck. One day a BOAC captain, after take-off from Goose Bay, made the sad discovery that the food had still not been upgraded. Justifiably irate the captain dashed off a report guaranteed to sizzle Mr. Duck's feathers and ending with this line: "Surely this must forever cook Duck's goose at Gander!"

* * *

In Chapter IX of this book we wrote about the extraordinarily strong winds consistently being battled by Loganair, the Orkney Islands airline.

The story brings to mind an incident involving a cyclonic-force breeze encountered by United Air Lines Captain Jack Knight when he was just plain Jack Knight, airmail pilot for the U.S. Post Office Department.

The year was 1921. Knight had taken off from the Cheyenne field on his regular run to Salt Lake. At least that is where he thought he was going. He got his mail-loaded Liberty-powered DeHaviland biplane up to 600 feet, flew wide open for one and one-half hours and never got out of sight of the field. The wind was blowing a mere 125 miles an hour. When Knight finally decided he was getting nowhere fast, he returned to the Cheyenne field.

It took him two minutes!

* * *

Have you ever heard of an airplane engine being tarred and feathered? It happened!

Captain Tex Guthrie, who naturally hails from the Lone Star State, was flying a Constellation one day when his number 3 engine started acting up and losing power.

Picking up his radio mike, Guthrie advised Air Traffic Control he was returning because his number 3 engine 'was tarred and feathered." Asked for an explanation, Guthrie replied:

"Well, it just got tarred (Texan for tired), and I feathered it."

Perhaps you've heard of the exploits of that great Chinese pilot, One Wing Low. Perhaps not. At any rate, Low notwithstanding, there were these United Air Lines pilots Lee and Hoy—Captain E. Hamilton Lee and First Officer Ed Hoy, that is. Well, according to UAL's Brownie Gray, Lee and Hoy were flying a trip from Cheyenne to Omaha. One of their passengers happened to be movie star Myrna Loy. Now what could be more fascinating than an episode involving a Lee, a Hoy and a Loy?

The weather was stinking; not an entirely unusual situation across Wyoming and Nebraska. In fact it stunk so bad that Lee and Hoy had it "up to here" with the weather and landed at Sidney, Nebraska, not exactly famous as a metropolitan center.

Miss Loy, noting that they had not landed at Omaha, summoned the stewardess and demanded to know what they were doing on the ground at only God-knows-where, and who were the pilots anyway?

Informed they had landed at Sidney and the pilots were Lee and Hoy, she exploded:

"Well, what can you expect from a couple of Chinamen anyway!"

* * *